DO THE WORK!

AN ANTIRACIST ACTIVITY BOOK

W. KAMAU BELL & KATE SCHATZ

WORKMAN PUBLISHING · NEW YORK

Library of Congress Cataloging-in-Publication Data is available.

ISBN 978-1-5235-1428-1

Design by Dian Holton
Cover illustration by Marcus Kwame Anderson
Illustrations by

Adriana Bellet	Jade Schulz	Martin Gee	Simone Martin-Newberry
Harkiran Kalsi	Keisha Okafor	Nicole Miles	
Hye Jin Chung	Kruttika Susarla	Paola Sorto	Susana Sanchez
Hyesu Lee	Marcus Kwame Anderson	Salini Perera	Therrious Davis
Favianna Rodriguez			

For permissions list please see page 160.

Workman books are available at special discounts when purchased in bulk
for premiums and sales promotions as well as for fundraising or educational use.
Special editions or book excerpts can also be created to specification.
For details, contact the Special Sales Director at specialmarkets@workman.com.

Workman Publishing Co., Inc.
225 Varick Street
New York, NY 10014-4381
workman.com

WORKMAN is a registered trademark of Workman Publishing Co., Inc.

Printed in China
First printing July 2022

10 9 8 7 6 5 4 3 2 1

Okay.

So let me get this straight—you mean to tell me there's a practical guide for how to fight back against all the things we hate about the world, and build the world we deserve? Seriously? Yo, sign me up!

All jokes aside (that one's for you, Kamau), *Do the Work!* could not have come at a better time. As someone who has worked tirelessly to build power for Black communities so that we can be powerful in every aspect of our lives, I know a few things for sure.

One, we can't leave things up to someone else. It's life or death right now, and that's really not a joke. Democracy is crumbling before our eyes, the planet is on fire, our communities don't have what we need to live well, and the gap between those who have and those who don't is growing deeper and wider every day. No one is coming to save us—it's time to save ourselves and take our communities back.

Two, everyone has a role to play. Not someone who wants to or can join a protest? Picket signs just not your thing? That's okay! It's great, actually, because we need people who will do more than that anyway. Protest is just one piece of the puzzle—we need people in every sector, every workplace, every state, every household to take up something. If you're a teacher, use your skills for change! If you commandeer a cash register like nobody's business, or make sure that the floors are clean for customers, we need your skills to create change! Everyone has a role to play, and all you gotta know how to do is to keep coming back to do more. This book will give you the rest.

Three, there is absolutely room for waking among the woke. Every single one of us who has done something to change society started off knowing nothing about how to do that. I used to believe that there were people without homes because they didn't work hard enough. I had a lot of beliefs and values that I had to unlearn before I could learn how to change things. I had people who knew a little bit more than I did who took me under their wings and helped explain things to me. We have all been there. You don't have to know everything before you can make a change. You don't have to do things perfectly to make change. You just have to be willing to learn, and to try.

Consider this your golden invitation to join a movement that will make all of us better, and our world a more just, fair, and safe place. We're so grateful that you're here! Now, let's get to work.

Alicia Garza

WELCOME TO
DO THE WORK!

WKB: We're here to talk to you—and to each other—about doing the work.

KS: About being less racist and more effective, informed humans.

WKB: About what "the work" actually *is* . . .

KS: . . . and what it can look, feel, and sound like when you actually do it.

WKB: This is a workbook. It's meant to be picked up, put down, carried around, ripped apart, played with, shared, and absorbed.

KS: We want you to write in it. Write all over it. Rip out pages and put them on your fridge!

WKB: Think of this book as a companion to the incredible work that is already being done (including all the antiracist books you bought for your book club), intended to inspire you to move from "What can I do?" to, you know, actually doing the *work*. Think of it as a bridge between the essential reading and the critical action.

KS: There are history lessons and quizzes! Activities, games, and crossword puzzles! And prompts to help you get real deep and real *real* about your own experiences with race, racism, and white supremacy.

WKB: And there are jokes! Because racism is so hilarious! And coloring pages, because come on, we need some joy, too.

KS: We will definitely end racism by telling jokes and coloring.

WKB: As parents, we know that games and activities are fun and often unexpected ways to learn new things. And all the other ways that we've been trying to get people to stop being racist aren't working out so well. We clearly need some additional tactics.

KS: Here's what else we put in this book: *a lot* of information.

WKB: Things They Never Taught You In History Class But Really Should Have Because If They Did Maybe We Wouldn't Be In This Mess.

KS: We need to understand what lies beneath this nation, and within ourselves: all the histories and systems that got us to where we are today. If we don't, our work will be less effective.

WKB: That's a nice white way of saying it'll be some bullshit. (But if you want to skip ahead to the part where we give you a bunch of ideas for what to actually *do*, see Chapter 4.)

KS: FYI: We swear sometimes.

WKB: It's true. Because sometimes the only way to really express how we feel about white supremacy is to

KS: We realize that all this content might seem . . . overwhelming. And intimidating.

WKB: Which may be true for some readers. It *is* a lot—but it's also nowhere near enough. What we cover here is just the tip of the white supremacy iceberg (for more on icebergs and white supremacy, see page 37). The full scope of hundreds of years of oppression and violence just can't be contained in one single book.

KS: At least not a book of this length. Our editor insisted that it couldn't be 10,000 pages.

WKB: So think of it like an overview! A Racism Sampler Platter paired with a Flight of Ideas For How *You* Can Take Action.

KS: Speaking of hundreds of years of oppression and violence, before we go any further we would like to acknowledge that this book was written on the unceded land of the Ohlone people.

WKB: Where are you reading it? Do you know whose land you're on?

KS: Let's find out. . . .

Please read these books! For a full list of titles and authors see the DO THE READING list on page 152.

Upper Tanana

Unangam Tanangin
(Unangax̂ /Aleut)

Gitanyow Lax'yip

St'aschinuw
(Naskapi)

Beothuk

Twana/Skokomish Sisseton

Takelma

Omaha

Pawtucket

Kiowa-Comanche-
Apache (Oklahoma)

Tequesta

Kō Hawai'i Pae'āina
(Hawaiian Kingdom)

Guachichil

Ciguayo

Chorotega

Whose Land Are You On?

Unless you have Indigenous ancestry, you're on stolen land—no matter where you live and how long your family has been there. America's white supremacist settler colonialism starts with the theft of indigenous land, and the attempted erasure of the people living on it.

A *land acknowledgement* is a way to recognize the Indigenous peoples who are the original stewards of the lands we're on. It can be a short statement ("This book was written on Ohlone land") or a more detailed explanation:

> **Horše ṭuuxi!** *This book was written on the territory of xučyun (Huichin), the ancestral and unceded land of the Chochenyo-speaking Ohlone people, the successors of the sovereign Verona Band of Alameda County. This land was and continues to be of great importance to the Muwekma Ohlone Tribe and other familial descendants of the Verona Band.*

While more non-Indigenous people and even some governments (including New Zealand and Canada) are incorporating land acknowledgements into public events and meetings, it's important to note that this is a long-standing practice of respect in many Indigenous nations and communities. When non-Indigenous people engage in this practice, it is one small step toward creating awareness of Indigenous communities and reminding people that they were here long before we were—and they're still here now.

A REMINDER
When talking about Indigenous people, use past, present, and future tenses. Indigenous people are not a relic of the past— they are alive, and thriving. This exercise is just a small step toward understanding and acknowledging the histories and futures of Indigenous communities, and your relationships to them.

DO THE WORK

To find out whose land you're on, and to learn more about Indigenous customs, languages, and contemporary life, please stop reading this book and visit the website native-land.ca.

Enter your zip code, do some reading, and then come back and complete the following questions:

What is the **traditional Indigenous** name of the land you're on?

How do you pronounce it? If you're not sure, do your best to find out.

How and when was the land colonized?

Does the Indigenous community have an active presence in your area? Do they have a website? A call for a land tax? Find out!

We asked **Sadie Red Wing**, a Lakota and Dakota graphic designer and educator, to help us imagine what it might look like if honoring Indigenous land was just what we did.

LOOK IT UP!
- #LandBack Movement
- Settler Colonialism
- Tribal Sovereignty
- Land Acknowledgement

Your turn: Draw another land acknowledgment scene.

How to Use This Book

How you approach the book is up to you—read each page in order, or go for the Choose-Your-Own-Adventure method. But no matter how you proceed, we hope you take your time. There's no rush (aside from the urgent need to dismantle white supremacy). It's OK to be thorough and slow.

These are cartoon versions of us by artist Marcus Kwame Anderson (in real life, we're less adorable). We'll be your chatty guides throughout the book.

The DO THE WORK icon lets you know you've got an assignment (or two).

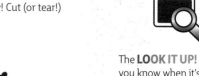

Throughout the book you'll find icons letting you know which supplies you'll need! Some activities are made to be removed from the book. If it's perforated, don't be shy! Cut (or tear!) it out.

Our names are on the cover, but we didn't write this book by ourselves. We include ideas and art from all kinds of super-smart, super-talented creators and contributors (and yes, we paid them). You'll find out more about them at the end of the book!

The DO THE READING icon lets you know we're recommending a book or an essay.

The **LOOK IT UP!** icon lets you know when it's time for you to look something up on your own (instead of asking others to explain it, or waiting to be told). Doing the work means getting curious, and doing your research.

In the back of the book you'll find stickers, answers to puzzles and quizzes, and more.

Who is this book for?

THIS BOOK IS FOR WHITE PEOPLE.

Let's just own that right off the bat. When it comes to identifying and dismantling white supremacy in America, the primary group of people who need to read a book about how to do that work are white people. Period.

That said: **This book is not just for white people.** White supremacy messes with *all* of us. We can *all* use ideas and tools for dismantling it, and for effectively showing up for our communities and others. While some sections of this book are directly addressed to white readers, we wrote it knowing that *anyone* could be reading and listening. And everyone has a lot to learn and to think about. For those of us who aren't white: When we take the time to consider each other's histories and experiences, we become better equipped to have nuanced conversations, and build stronger coalitions. We hope that all readers feel seen and respected in these pages.

THIS BOOK IS ALSO FOR PEOPLE WHO ...

- Know the system's broken—but aren't sure how to fix it or rebuild it entirely.
- Learned more over the summer by doing the activity workbooks than they did during the actual school year.
- Enjoy crosswords, games, *and* antiracist ideas, and have been waiting to enjoy them at the same time.
- Were shocked that the United States of America elected Donald Trump and want to make sure it never happens again.
- Were not shocked by that election (and want to make sure it never happens again).
- Go to protests and afterward think to themselves "What next?"
- Didn't think much about racism and police violence until the deaths of George Floyd, Breonna Taylor, and Ahmaud Arbery. Or Tony McDade, or Sean Monterrosa. Or Rekia Boyd or Korryn Gaines. Philando Castile and Michael Brown. Sandra Bland and Eric Garner. Freddie Gray and Jordan Davis. Aiyana Stanley-Jones and Trayvon Martin and Tamir Rice. Oscar Grant, Sean Bell . . .
- Just read that list and realized they'd only heard of some of those names—and will now look up the ones they don't know.
- Already know much of what is in this book but want help explaining what they know to the people who don't know.

Any of this sound familiar? This book's for you.

Why do we use the words we use?

Throughout the book we use specific terms and acronyms to refer to groups of people. This is a necessary part of writing a book like this—because, words. It's also challenging and imperfect—also because, words.

Fear of using the wrong words can often hold folks back from talking about race. That's a legit fear. These words are constantly evolving, getting embraced, then getting challenged, then evolving again. Not everyone agrees on every term. Not everyone in a racial or an ethnic group likes the same identifier, or wants their complex existence to be reduced at all. As marginalized communities assert the power to self-define, form new alliances, and leverage political power, we all get to collectively grapple with the complexities of what and who we are, and how to talk about it all.

And that's all good!

We think adrienne maree brown said it best in the introduction to her book *Pleasure Activism* (a book we highly recommend): "If this is being read in a future in which this language has evolved, then please know I would be evolving right along with you."

THROUGHOUT THE BOOK WE USE:

• **AAPI:** Asian American and Pacific Islander.

• **BIPOC:** Black, Indigenous, People of Color. It's not a perfect term—acronyms are reductive on purpose. But they save space in a book where word count matters!

• **Black with a capital "B":** The capital "B" acknowledges being "Black" isn't just a description of skin color, it is a distinct identity with cultures and traditions. It's an acknowledgement of the fact Black people have fought for that acknowledgement.

• **Indigenous and Native:** The original people of this land should be referred to by their tribal groups whenever possible. When referring to the whole racial group there is not unified agreement on a term, but *Indigenous* and *Native* are generally used most often.

• **Latino/a:** Some folks prefer the gender-neutral term Latinx; because this is a relatively new term that doesn't have a broad consensus for usage, we're using a combination of suffixes when the gender is not specified.

• **MENA:** Middle Eastern and North African.

• **People of color:** This has generally referred to all people who aren't white. We use it here when our eyes are tired of seeing BIPOC, and when we're not specifically talking about Black folks.

• **white with a lowercase "w":** *Heavy sigh.* See below. . . .

THIS IS KAMAU. CAN I HAVE A BRIEF SIDEBAR?

So Black writers, academics, journalists, tweeters, and more fought for yeeeeeeears to get "Black" a capital "B." We fought with editors, other academics, internet trolls, and grammarians (amateur and professional). I know this because I was one of those Black writers who fought this battle. I had editors lowercase my capital "B"s regularly.

And the mostly white decision makers only allowed the capital "B" version of "Black" after the murder of George Floyd and the ensuing world-shaking events. Hooray for that! But then those same decision makers just quietly went ahead and started capitalizing the "w" in "white." From "white people" to "White people." And honestly it felt like "WHITE PEOPLE!" Black people kicked down the door, and then white people just sauntered on through it . . . and they didn't even ask for it. Just a few of them had to stick their pointer fingers up in the air and go, "Well, actually. . . ."

To us, that just feels wrong. So our "w" is lowercase. That all being said, if you want *white* capitalized, we understand. This is a literal workbook: Use your pens and pencils and in the paraphrased words of Marcus Garvey . . .

"Uppercase! Uppercase! You whitey race!"

And why, exactly, should you listen to us?

WKB: Excellent question. You can't trust just anyone these days.

KS: Hopefully you're listening to multiple people, not just us. If you're white, please make sure that you're listening to *way* more people of color.

WKB: We're two writer/creative types who live in the part of the San Francisco Bay Area affectionately known as "the East Bay." Both of our careers are in some way or another about dismantling white supremacy.

KS: Kamau does it with humor and documentaries and television and Twitter.

WKB: Kate does it by writing feminist children's books and researching lesser-known radical histories, and by constantly pulling white people aside to say, "Ummm . . . maybe don't do that."

KS: We both have a lot of experience thinking and talking and writing about race and racism—

WKB: I even have experience experiencing it!

KS: A literal expert! My expertise is being raised in a white supremacist culture that's always placed people who look like me in the center of everything. And trying to figure out how to unlearn that.

WKB: Another thing we have in common is that people often come to us asking, "What do I do about racial injustice?"

KS: Specifically, white people ask us that.

WKB: *Lots* of white people.

KS: Let's be super clear about something: *It's an incredibly important question.* When you ask "what do I dooooo?" it shows that you give a shit.

WKB: That you know something's not right.

KS: This reminds me of the antiracist educator Jane Elliott. There's an exercise she does with the non-Black members of her audiences.

WKB: Are we gonna do it with our readers?

KS: Yup. She's onstage, and she tells the crowd: "Think very carefully about the ways in which Black Americans are treated."

WKB: Are you thinking?

KS: She says, "Think about *all* the treatment, within *all* of the systems—from schools to healthcare to housing to policing and prisons."

WKB: Keep thinking . . .

KS: Then she says: "If you would be happy to wake up tomorrow and receive the same treatment as your Black friends, neighbors, and coworkers, please stand up."

WKB: I bet nobody stands up.

KS: No one in her audiences stands up. No one *ever* stands up.

WKB: Damn. What does Jane do with that?

KS: She says, "The fact that no one stood up tells me that every single one of you knows exactly what is happening. You *all* know and see the problem. So *what* are you doing about it?"

WKB: And there you have it, folks! *That's* what it's all about. That's what the work is. Now let's do it.

SHE DID THE WORK!

Jane Elliott did the work when she conducted her now-famous "Blue Eyes/Brown Eyes" exercise with her elementary school students in April of 1968, after they asked questions about the murder of Dr. Martin Luther King Jr. To help the children understand the unfairness and pain of racial discrimination, she decided to separate them based on eye color. For several days she switched between treating the two groups as superior, and then had the students write reflections on the experience. Their insights and the experiment gained national media attention, and Jane Elliott appeared on *The Tonight Show with Johnny Carson*. She received severe backlash, and was shunned by all but one of her colleagues. She continued to develop the exercise, eventually using it with adults—it is now considered one of the earliest methods of diversity training in the workplace.

Understanding race, racism, and white supremacy begins with understanding your own relationships to it all. Let's start with exploring how we identify—and what has shaped those identities over time. **We'll go first:**

NAME **W. KAMAU BELL**

HOW I IDENTIFY

- If you stopped me on the street and said, "QUICK! HOW DO YOU IDENTIFY?" I'd probably answer, "BlackMale," as if it was one word. Or maybe "Big BlackMale."
- If I was filling out my "Racial LinkedIn," I'd say "A big, tall, Black comedian who's also a heterosexual, cisgender, crybaby, easily distracted, politically progressive family man."

WHO I COME FROM

- My parents are Janet Cheatham Bell and Walter Bell.
- Like most Black Americans I can trace my family tree back to slavery and not before.
- My dad is an inside agitator and my mom is an outside agitator. I joke that I'm from a mixed marriage. My dad is Black, and my mother is BLACK!
- My dad has traveled the world for work but has lived most of his life in Mobile, AL. He loves the South: He understands its faults and constantly works to make it better.
- My mom grew up in Indianapolis, IN, a good ol' KKK stronghold. My mom was among the first Black students to integrate her high school. She does not have many good things to say about Indiana.
- My parents are high achievers. Because of when and where they were born they were both often the first Black people ever to do whatever they were doing. And they did a damn good job, no matter what it was.

WHERE I'VE LIVED

- Growing up, I moved around a lot with my mom. We lived in so many places: East Palo Alto, CA; Indianapolis, IN; Boston, MA.
- I also spent time with my dad in Mobile, AL.
- On my own I've lived in Chicago, IL; Philadelphia, PA; San Francisco, CA; New York, NY; Berkeley, CA; and Oakland, CA.

HOW I WAS EDUCATED

- Elementary School: It was a mix of public, private, and occasionally Catholic schools. But mostly, private schools, which of course means overwhelmingly whiiiiiite!
- College: I went to an Ivy League school, dropped out of an Ivy League school, went to a media arts school and dropped out of that too. I think my biggest college accomplishment was reading *The Autobiography of Malcolm X*. Not for a class, but because the movie was about to come out.

WHAT I DO FOR WORK

- I'm a comedian, TV host, writer, producer, and director who tries to make all of his projects as entertaining and antiracist as possible. I'm always trying to figure out how to work with power in order to make real change (while knowing that you can't expect the halls of power to give up that power, and that much of the change has to come from the outside). Basically, I'm the guy who talked to the KKK on CNN.

WHO MY PEOPLE ARE

- I'm married to Melissa Hudson Bell, a white woman who mostly connects with her Sicilian and Irish heritage. She is a doctor of dance. Literally. She has a PhD in Critical Dance Studies. We have been together since 2003. And she has been calling "Karens" out on their shit since way before it was cool.
- We have three Black and mixed race daughters who have three different shades of skin and three different types of hair.

I FIRST REALIZED I WAS BLACK WHEN

I would imagine that it would be hard for most Black people to remember this specific moment. We always need to know that we are Black, because so much of how we are treated by this country is based on that. My mom told me a story about how, when I was a toddler, she stopped a white man from rubbing my head for good luck. I also have vivid memories of being in a drug store with my mom and her pointing out the man who was following us around to make sure we didn't steal. She made it clear he was doing that because we were Black.

NAME **Kate Schatz**

HOW I IDENTIFY
White, cisgender, queer, American woman. Left-handed lesbian, vegetarian rabble-rouser. Mother, daughter, partner. Author, writer, talker, activist. Professional feminist, amatuer historian.

WHO I COME FROM
- A long line of white people, including loving, hardworking, still-married hippie parents; a car salesman grandpa; an art teacher grandma; and lots of rock-n-roller counterculture aunts, uncles, and half-siblings.
- My German ancestry is the closest I've come to an ethnic identity. My paternal great-grandfather came to San Francisco from Germany in the late 1800s to make beer, and my Grandpa Hans spoke German to me as a kid.
- The other branches of my family came from Sweden, Ireland, and Scotland along with millions of others in the nineteenth century.
- I've found records of ancestors who fought in the Revolutionary War, as well as the Civil War—for the Union and the Confederacy. I've also found census records for two enslaver ancestors from Kentucky.

WHERE I'VE LIVED
- Born and raised in San Jose, CA—same house my entire life. Upbringing was working-middle class. Not rich or fancy but comfortable and stable. San Jose is racially diverse, but most communities I was part of as a child were predominantly white.
- I moved to Oakland, CA, in my twenties, and it was the first time that I lived and worked among a significant Black population.
- I lived in Santa Cruz, CA, for undergrad, and Providence, RI, for grad school. Both super white cities, but in very different ways. I vastly prefer sunshine and the Pacific Ocean.
- I've never lived in a neighborhood or community where I felt unsafe or unwelcome or Other. I'm conscious of how this has informed—and limited—my perspectives.

HOW I WAS EDUCATED
- Local public schools. My schools weren't majority white, but most of my classes were: I was tracked into "gifted" programs, while many of my Mexican, Vietnamese, and Filipino peers were tracked into ESL and "remedial" classes.
- Self-education happened in middle and high school: went vegetarian, declared myself a feminist, fell in love with a girl, attended pro-choice marches, read Howard Zinn. High school and college were where my feminist education began.
- At UC Santa Cruz I majored in Women's Studies and Creative Writing, and was able to learn from the exact kind of amazing radical lefty professors your parents warned you about.

WHAT I DO FOR WORK
- I write books about radical women and cool histories and tell stories that don't get told as often as they should.
- I go down research rabbit holes and emerge with engaging stories that I love to share.
- I speak to audiences about feminism and history, and politics and activism, and whiteness and racism and antiracism.

WHO MY PEOPLE ARE
- I've been lucky to work, learn, and create alongside many BIPOC activists, scholars, and artists who've shaped my education around race, white supremacy, and my own relationship to all of it.
- I live with my partner, Lauren, our three children, and many pets. She's white, from Texas, and we both answer proudly to gay, lesbian, and/or queer (though we mostly answer to "MOM!" yelled loudly from another room). Our community includes fellow queer families, many neighbors and friends, and our kids' dads, with whom we lovingly co-parent.
- I'm an extrovert who's good at staying in touch. I know a lot of fascinating people and love nothing more than bringing them together and connecting them to each other.

I FIRST REALIZED I WAS WHITE WHEN
I first realized I was white at my high school's info night for prospective parents. I was on a student panel, and the white parents kept asking my white friend and me pointed—but coded—questions about the school's "diversity" and "gang activity." I realized that they saw me as "like them," and my Latino/a and Asian peers as potential threats to their kids. I became aware of my whiteness, and I was pissed. That moment changed me.

Your Turn!

HOW I IDENTIFY

WHO I COME FROM

WHERE I'VE LIVED

HOW I WAS EDUCATED

WHAT I DO FOR WORK

WHO MY PEOPLE ARE

I FIRST REALIZED I WAS _____ WHEN

Doing the Work is _____

We asked folks from our communities and they said:

Doing the Work is ___imperative___

Doing the Work is ___OUR ONLY WAY FORWARD___

Doing the Work is ___Sometimes difficult and uncomfortable___

Doing the Work is ___WORTH IT___

Doing the Work is ___Quiet, sometimes; lonely, sometimes. And that's okay.___

Doing the Work is ___INTENSE___

Doing the Work is ___a mixture of big and small actions wherever you see opportunities___

Doing the Work is ___never finished___

Doing the Work is ___Work. LITERAL Work.___

Doing the Work is ___STRUCTURAL___

Doing the Work is ___listening___

Doing the Work is ___Giving up power, Resource, Land, and Control___

Doing the Work is ___Staying engaged in politics___

Doing the Work is ___how we build the world we want to see___

Doing the Work is ___GENERATIONAL___

Doing the Work is ___Examining your own shit___

Doing the Work is ___urgent. Messy. Necessary. forever.___

Doing the Work is ___the most important job___

Doing the Work is ___Better than being an asshole!___

Doing the Work is ___reparations___

Doing the Work is ___heartbreaking___

Doing the Work is ___MORE IMPACTFUL THAN TALKING THE TALK___

Doing the Work is ___Not optional___

Doing the Work is ___Terrifying but absolutely Necessary___

Doing the Work is ___Sparking suprising and difficult Conversations with my kids.___

Doing the Work is ___The Joy!___

CHAPTER

1

Let's Talk About It

Let's start doing the work by getting on the same page. In this chapter we'll:

➡️ Look at what race, racism, and white supremacy even are, and define the terms we'll be using throughout the book.

➡️ Explore why it's hard to talk about it, for white people AND for BIPOC folks.

➡️ Review some of greatest hits of defensive white people.

➡️ Practice spotting the racist BS that surrounds us.

➡️ Get into what it means to be antiracist.

➡️ Do the work by getting on the same page.

SUPPLIES

PEN/PENCIL · ART SUPPLIES · INTERNET · SCISSORS

PLEASE COMPLETE THE FOLLOWING QUESTIONS BEFORE PROCEEDING TO CHAPTER ONE

1. Which of the following is a right guaranteed by the Bill of Rights?

_____ Public Education   _____ Employment

_____ Trial by Jury   _____ Voting

2. The federal census of population is taken every five years.

_____ True   _____ False

3. If a person is indicted for a crime, name two rights that they have.

_____

4. A US senator elected at the general election in November takes office the following year on what date?

_____

5. A president elected at the general election in November takes office the following year on what date?

_____

6. Which definition applies to the word "amendment"?

_____ Proposed change, as in the Constitution

_____ Making peace between nationals at war

_____ A part of the government

7. A person appointed to the US Supreme Court is appointed for a term of _____.

8. When the Constitution was approved by the original colonies, how many states had to ratify it in order

for it to be in effect? _____

9. Does enumeration affect the income tax levied on citizens in various states? _____

10. A person opposed to swearing in an oath may say, instead: _____.

I (solemnly) _____

11. To serve as President of the United States, a person must have attained:

_____ 25 years of age   _____ 35 years of age   _____ 40 years of age   _____ 45 years of age

12. What words are required by law to be on all coins and paper currency of the United States?

_____

13. The Supreme Court is the chief lawmaking body of the state.

_____ True   _____ False

14. If a law passed by a state is contrary to provisions of the US Constitution, which law prevails?

_____

15. If a vacancy occurs in the US Senate, the state must hold an election, but meanwhile the place may be

filled by a temporary appointment made by _____

Good job!

You just answered the first 15 (of 68) questions from the state of Alabama's Literacy Test from 1965, the same year that Literacy Tests were finally eliminated by the Civil Rights Act. Literacy Tests came into use in many Southern states at the end of the nineteenth century, and were one of several voter suppression tactics in the century-long effort to discourage, intimidate, and disenfranchise Black and poor voters. Other tactics included grandfather clauses, poll taxes, intimidation, and lynching and other forms of physical violence.

Tests were administered to individuals attempting to register to vote, and were given at the arbitrary (and usually racist) discretion of the County Clerk. If a clerk wanted a person to be able to register, he could just ask one question to "prove" that the person was literate enough to vote. A common, easy question to give to a white applicant was "Who is the president of the United States?" If the clerk decided to give you this test (because you were Black, or a poor white laborer), you had a limited amount of time to complete it, which was also up to the clerk. If you missed more than 7 of the 68 questions, your application—and your right to vote—would be denied.

How did you do? Would you have been able to register to vote?

Let's talk about race. Specifically, why it is so hard for white people to talk about it. Kate, can you explain?

Yes! I have ALL the answers! Just kidding. But I do have some ideas, based on my experiences as a white person, and the many conversations I've had with other white people about it.

WKB: Cool. Ideas are fine. I'll take anything if it'll help me understand!

KS: White people don't like to talk about race because it's hard. And we don't like when things are hard. We're afraid of getting it wrong. Of being the bad guy. Of saying the wrong thing. Of having to own our own shit. We get defensive and awkward, angry and indignant. We feel blamed and guilty. Because white supremacy has taught us that we are the center of it all—and talking openly and honestly about race threatens that precarious illusion. And when that happens, we tend to get reaaaaal messy.

WKB: And in the process of all this drama, you end up making it seem like "being white" is harder than "being Black." Like rich people who say bullshit like "Money doesn't equal happiness," or "Mo' money. Mo' problems." (Damn, now that song's stuck in my head.)

KS: We're so scared of being blamed, and having to accept our shortcomings and failures, that we often make ourselves the victim.

WKB: I don't think that white people actually talk to other white people about race in any kind of substantive way. And if they talk to Black people about race, they treat it like they're giving us a gift. But it's a gift we didn't ask for. Like a tuna noodle casserole at a barbecue. Take that shit home and eat it with your people.

KS: Most white people just don't know how. We think we're not supposed to mention it. If we're not raised to be straight-up racists, we're raised to think it's rude to even mention race, that the opposite of being racist is being "color-blind." So a huge part of white people getting better at talking about race is just learning that it's OK to ask questions, to re-educate ourselves. It's OK to be uncomfortable.

WKB: Since you mentioned that it's OK to ask questions . . . there's a lot of stuff I still don't understand about white people.

KS: Go for it.

WKB: Disclaimer: I know nothing is completely true about any group of people. OK?

KS: Gotcha. #NotAllWhitePeople.

WKB: Why don't white people use washcloths when they take baths or showers?

KS: Do loofahs count?

WKB: And why so many casseroles?

KS: Wait, Black people don't eat casseroles? I'm learning so much here.

WKB: And why don't white men use lotion on their whole bodies?

KS: Ew. They really should. And I have to admit, despite my full-on whiteness, these are mysteries to me as well. I blame my California hippie upbringing—I've never really had a casserole, and all my bathing involved washcloths drenched in Dr. Bronner's.

WKB: Also: Why are white people so obsessed with Dr. Bronner's?

KS: Now that's an excellent question. I love the stuff. Peppermint forever! White people don't often think of ourselves as racialized—we don't have to. In America, we are the default. We're the faces on TV, in the ads, in the history books, in the fairy tales.

WKB: You can just cruise on through the world without thinking about how your skin color, your names, your hair, your voices, are perceived. When your experience is the norm, you don't have to think about it. Nondisabled folks don't have to wonder whether or not an event will be wheelchair-accessible. Straight couples don't scan the street for threats before holding hands with their partners.

KS: When it comes to talking about racism, it's usually framed in terms of individual actions, rather than systemic and structural issues that we're all part of. This makes it easy for white people who consider ourselves not racist to compartmentalize racism as a bad thing that happens to other people who are not like us, perpetrated by other people who are not like us, because we don't do those things. We distance ourselves from it, and deny responsibility. That's why I'm using words like "we" and "us"—just because I'm writing this book doesn't mean I operate outside the damage of whiteness.

WKB: You *should* all be ashamed of yourselves. Completely and utterly ashamed. And instead of turning away from it like white people do when they feel shame, you should all stare at it and figure out how to deal with it. Stop acting like your shit don't stink, when it stinks even worse from all the casseroles.

KS: Not even the strongest Dr. Bronner's can cover it up. We have to talk about it! To each other. A white woman once asked me if it was problematic for white people to talk to each other about racism. "What if men were getting together to talk about ending the patriarchy?" she exclaimed in disbelief. I was like "Ma'am, when men start doing that I will be thrilled. I will find out where they're meeting, and send some damn flowers."

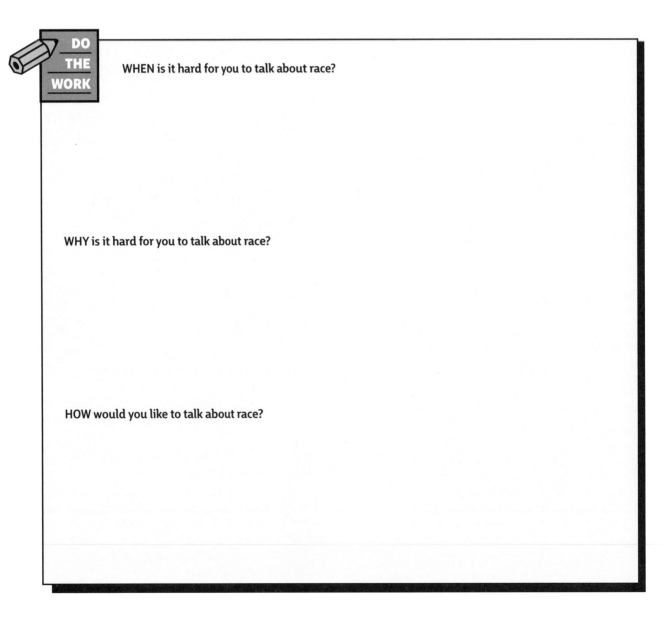

DO THE WORK

WHEN is it hard for you to talk about race?

WHY is it hard for you to talk about race?

HOW would you like to talk about race?

POP QUIZ! WHAT DO YOU KNOW ABOUT RACE?

1. In 2003, a team of scientists finished mapping the human genome. Of the approximately 20,500 human genes they identified, how many determine a person's race?

- ○ 17
- ○ 10,250
- ○ Inconclusive
- ○ 0
- ○ 2,358

2. Race is _____ . *(Check all that you believe to be true.)*

- ○ A social construct used throughout history to divide people into groups ranked as superior and inferior and to justify systems of power, privilege, and disenfranchisement
- ○ A biological reality proven by centuries of scientific research
- ○ A group of people sharing a common cultural, geographical, linguistic, or religious origin or background
- ○ An empowering way to understand my identity
- ○ Not that big a deal
- ○ A really big deal

3. One sure way you can identify someone's race is by…

- ○ Looking at them
- ○ Asking to see pictures of their parents
- ○ Dancing with them
- ○ Believing them when they tell you
- ○ Um … ermmm …

4. Which of the following terms have appeared on the US Census as categories for identity?

- ○ Slave
- ○ Quadroon
- ○ Hawaiian
- ○ Negro
- ○ Octoroon
- ○ Indian
- ○ Hindu
- ○ Native American
- ○ Mulatto
- ○ Mexican
- ○ All of the above

5. What race is The Rock?

- ○ Wait … The Rock's not white?
- ○ Black
- ○ Samoan
- ○ Black and Samoan
- ○ Who cares? He's Box Office Gold

6. The racial category of "Caucasian" comes from:

- ○ Greek philosopher Aristotle
- ○ Eighteenth-century anthropologist Johann Friedrich Blumenbach
- ○ The Caucasian Brothers, a nineteenth-century American vaudeville act
- ○ Thomas Jefferson
- ○ The myth of Prometheus

7. Jewish people are white.
- ○ True
- ○ False

BONUS QUESTION FOR WHITE READERS!

Complete the sentence: Whiteness is …

_____

_____

_____

_____

ANSWERS

1. The answer is "0." As in none. As in: When the final analysis of the Human Genome Project (HGP) was complete, researchers confirmed that all humans on Earth are 99.9 percent genetically identical. Each human has 3 billion base pairs of genetic letters—and mine are 99.9 percent the same as yours.

Here's what the National Human Genome Institute has to say about race:

Race is a fluid concept used to group people according to various factors, including ancestral background and social identity. Race is also used to group people that share a set of visible characteristics, such as skin color and facial features. Though these visible traits are influenced by genes, the vast majority of genetic variation exists within racial groups and not between them. Race is an ideology and for this reason, many scientists believe that race should be more accurately described as a social construct and not a biological one.

2. Since this question is asking what you *believe* to be true, there are really no right or wrong answers. Our experiences with race are deeply personal. They're circumstantial, subjective, and nuanced. Race might be a huge part of your everyday experience—or it might be something

you've never really thought about until this very second.

However: B is *factually* wrong. As we just explained, race is not a scientific, biological, or genetic fact. While there are several centuries worth of scientific attempts to prove otherwise, the current understanding is that **race is a social construct**. As Dr. Nell Irvin Painter says in the introduction to her book *The History of White People*, race is "an idea, not a fact." Does that mean it's not a huge, important, consequential reality? Does that mean that *racial identity* isn't real? Does that mean we "don't see color"?! Nope, nope, and NOPE.

Does that mean that it's all pretty confusing? Yes, it absolutely is.

3. Believing what someone tells you is still the best way (despite what Rachel Dolezal did to ruin that). But, also, they have to tell of their own volition. You don't get to ask just because you're curious.

Pictures of peoples' parents? Nope. One word: adoption. Dancing? Come on! You're better than this.

Try as you might, you can't always be sure of a person's racial identity just by looking at them.

When it comes to "knowing" someone's race, the most important thing you need is, as New Edition's Ralph Tresvant put it, *sen-si-tiv-ity*. Because racial categorization is not

science. There are plenty of people who have been brought up being told they are one race only to find out later that they had been misled or there had been confusion about the family tree. (Thanks, at-home DNA services!) When that happens, what are those people supposed to do? Deny how they have been raised to identify? Or just be who they have always been to themselves and the world? No, seriously. We don't know the answer. We are asking you.

4. The answer is: All of the above. If you want to see how ideas about racial categorization shift over time, take a look at the history of the US census.

The first census, done in 1790, gave three options for who you were and how you'd be counted:

- Free white female or male
- All other free persons
- Slave

Since 1790, "white" has been the only consistent term on the census (it changed once, going from "Free white" to just "white" in 1850). By 1830, there was an option for "free colored persons." The 1870 census added "Chinese" as the first category based on nation of origin. By 1890, all Blacks were legally free, and were divided into four categories: "blacks," "mulattos," "quadroons," and "octoroons." Instructions for the 1890 census takers explained:

The word "black" should be used to describe those persons who have three-fourths or more black blood; "mulatto," those persons who have from three-eighths to five-eighths black blood; "quadroon," those persons who have one-fourth black blood; and "octoroons," those persons who have one-eighth or any trace of black blood.

In all, there have been nine different terms used to categorize Black Americans, and other categories have been renamed, removed, and added based on shifts in culture, politics, immigration, and economics. It's way too much to get into here, but let's just say: A deep dive into census history reveals how tenuous and temporary our categories really are.

5. Some of you knew that we'd have to talk about The Rock. The Rock is walking proof that racial categorization is not a science. When Dwayne "The Rock" Johnson was named People Magazine's Sexiest Man Alive in 2016, I thought to myself, "I bet some people think he's white." He's not. And I'm guessing this is still true, even though the name "Dwayne Johnson" is eleventh on the list of Blackest names ever.

Sean Porter and Dwayne "The Rock" Johnson

The Rock identifies as half Black and half Samoan. By America's "rules" that means he's Black. But because of his look, and because of his first career (professional wrestling, still a predominantly white industry), he was able to just be himself, The Rock, aka "The Jabroni-beatin', pie-eatin', Hell-raisin', trailblazin', People's Champ!"

I'm not accusing The Rock of hiding anything. He is very proud of who he is. His first wrestling moniker honored both his Black dad and his Samoan grandfather. But his racially ambiguous status gives him access that he wouldn't get otherwise. In fact, in 2006, The Rock starred in *Gridiron Gang*. It was based on a true story, and The Rock played Sean Porter, who in real life is a white man. And while

Hollywood throughout its history has cast white people to play every race, The Rock is one of the few people of color to go the other way. (For more on this, see Bruno Mars.)

6. Thanks to German scientist Johann Friedrich Blumenbach, millions of white people still find themselves checking the "Caucasian" box without being able to find the Caucasus region on a world map! Yes, Prometheus did get eagle-assaulted in the Caucasus mountains. Aristotle *was* a fan of slavery-justifying taxonomies. And Jefferson did oversee the first census in 1790, but he used the term "white"—five years before Johann coined "Caucasian."

Blumenbach was an Enlightenment thinker, one of many educated white European dudes who developed "rational" ideas around science, politics, law, and, yes, racial categorization. In the 1770s, he identified five categories of humans—Caucasian, Mongolian, Ethiopian, American, and Malay—based on his studies of anatomy, and his extensive human skull collection. The most beautiful skull, he decided, belonged to a woman from Georgia (the country, which is located in the Caucasus region). He figured all people born there must be beautiful and perfect like the skull, and he ranked Caucasian as the superior race. And so, several centuries later, white people check "Caucasian" when they fill out forms at the DMV.

7. No, not all Jewish people are white. Also: It's complicated! White Jews are white. But not all Jews are white. And not all Jewish people of European descent consider themselves white. The answer is actually . . . more questions! Like: What does it even mean to be white? What does it mean to be Jewish? Is it a race? An ethnicity? A religion? Heritage? Nationality? Culture? *How does any of this work?*

What is true: There are Jewish people all over the world, from all different backgrounds. In the United States, the

majority of Jewish people are Ashkenazi (of Eastern European descent), many of whom (but not all) identify as white. But a not-small percentage of the Jewish population is "racially and ethnically diverse." There are Jewish Americans of color whose families have been Jewish for generations, if not centuries. Ashkenazi Jews weren't considered white in America until the early twentieth century—like other European immigrant groups that faced discrimination and violence, they gave up key elements of their culture to assimilate and benefit from what American whiteness offered. And while becoming white offers a great deal, it doesn't protect against antisemitism—like, not at all. White nationalists see Jews as "other," and Jewish Americans report the second-highest numbers of hate crimes, after Black Americans. In 2019 alone there was a 56 percent increase in reported antisemitic assaults, with a daily average of six antisemitic incidents per day in the United States.

> **DO THE READING**
>
> • *The History of White People* by Dr. Nell Irvin Painter
>
> • *The 1619 Project* created by Nikole Hannah-Jones (check out the podcast as well!)

So if "race" is a social construct, who constructed it? And when? And like, who invented racism?

Once upon a time,

in 1607, Jamestown became the first permanent English settlement in the "New World" (to the peoples who already lived there, it wasn't new). The colonists, who came from England, hoped to find gold, but that didn't happen. To make money, they planted crops like tobacco and cotton. But they needed lots of people to work the fields.

KS: Would you like to hear a story about it?

WKB: Yes! Is it about history?

KS: Colonial US history, in fact. It's not the *whole* story, but it can tell us a lot about the construction of race, slavery, and freedom in the United States.

WKB: Is it the story with the pilgrims and that nice turkey dinner?

KS: No.

WKB: The one where the angry white dudes dump the tea?

KS: Nope, it's the story about how the white colonial landowners and politicians came up with racial categories and proto-segregationist laws in order to consolidate wealth and power, suppress interracial worker solidarity, and maintain a subservient Black labor class!

WKB: A classic!

KS: That never gets told!

WKB: FYI readers, we'll get into more history in Chapter 3. But this is pretty foundational, so we thought we'd get it in early.

KS: Now gather 'round and listen. . . .

The colonists thought they could force the local Indigenous people to do it, but the Indigenous people often fought back. So the colonists brought poor people from back home in England who could work as *indentured servants*. Though they looked like what we'd now call "white people," they weren't known as "white" back then. They were "Christians" or "Englishmen." They worked really hard, under terrible conditions, but the deal was they got to be free when their work contracts (aka *indentures*) expired.

In the year 1619, another group of "unfree" workers appeared when a Dutch ship called *White Lion* arrived near Jamestown. On board were men who'd been kidnapped from the part of Africa that is now called Angola. They were sold to the colonists, as part of the inhumane nightmare known as the *transatlantic slave trade*. At first, they were also considered indentured servants, with the promise of freedom once their contracts were up.

More people were stolen from West Africa, the Caribbean, and South America and sold into bondage to work the land the colonists stole from the people who lived there when they showed up. These people weren't

Legislating Race

 1660

Virginia states that European servants face extra punishment if they run away with "Negro" servants.

 1662

Virginia enacts *partus sequitur ventrem*: The status of a child is derived from the status of the mother. Slavery is now hereditary, even the offspring of free "Christian" men who rape "Negro" women are born into bondage.

 1664

Maryland declares lifelong servitude for all enslaved "Negro" people who are already enslaved. New York, New Jersey, the Carolinas, and Virginia all do the same.

 1664

Virginia rules that converting to Christianity is no longer a way to change the conditions of enslaved Indigenous people and "Negros."

1669

If an enslaved person resists his enslaver, the enslaver responds with force, and the enslaved person "should chance to die," it's not actually murder, and enslavers shall always be acquitted.

called "Black," but they also weren't referred to by their country or tribe of origin, like the Englishmen. They were "Negroes," "Indians," or "Mulattoes," the terms used then for people of mixed ancestry. In many cases they lived and worked alongside poor English and European servants. It was not uncommon for Negro and English servants to marry and have children.

Life in the early decades of the colonial United States was harsh for everyone, but it was most brutal for the indentured servants and workers. Most only lived for a few years after arrival in the colonies. But by the 1630s, this started to change. Life expectancy improved, and more servants were able to live out their indentures and get free.

This meant that there were Negroes and Mulattoes who bought land and began to build lives as free people. Some earned their freedom by converting to Christianity. Some even owned servants of their own. At the same time, fewer indentured servants were coming from Europe. The rich landowners needed to stay rich, which meant they needed a permanent labor force.

And this, dear readers, is where it began. Remember: Enslavement was not still based on race or skin color. It was not inherited, and it was not a permanent condition. Over the next few decades, the powerful men of Virginia created a series of new laws that divided the servant class on the basis of skin color and origin, laying the groundwork for American *chattel slavery* and new race-based categories.

In 1640,

a man named John Punch and two other indentured servants were caught trying to escape Virginia for Maryland. They were each charged with the same crime. The two Englishmen got four extra years of servitude. But the judge sentenced John, who was of African descent, to servitude "for the time of his natural life." It was the very first time that slavery became a lifelong condition.

And then came Bacon's Rebellion! (Which does not involve actual bacon.)

In 1676, angry servants of European and African descent banded together in Virginia. Led by Englishman Nathaniel Bacon, they blamed their troubles on local Indigenous nations and the rich colonial elite. They attacked Indigenous people and then marched on Jamestown. The governor fled in fear, and the multiracial mob set Jamestown on fire.

Bacon's Rebellion was eventually put down by the British Army, but it terrified the ruling class. The union of the African and European servants showed that the working class had the potential to unite and overthrow the colonies. The landowners and lawmakers wondered: *What can we do to stop this from happening again?*

The solution was to "divide and conquer" the European and African servants based on what they *didn't* have in common: their skin color. They created even more laws that made everything worse for the people of African descent—even the "free" ones who worked off their indentures!—while also creating laws that gave scraps of power to the European servants, putting them above Black servants in a new legal and social hierarchy. The status of Black men in Virginia shifted from indentured servants with a path to freedom to permanently enslaved.

The trade of enslaved people grew swiftly, and so did the laws connecting skin color to freedom. Five years after Bacon's Rebellion, in 1681, the word "white" first appeared in a legal US document: it was illegal for "a white man, a person of a race distinguished by a light complexion" to marry various categories of "non-whites." The word "white" soon replaced "Christian" and "English."

And so, by the beginning of the eighteenth century, almost one century into the American experiment, poor white people had more in common with the rich people who *looked* like them, rather than the other poor people who didn't. Their new status as "white" protected them from the horrors of chattel slavery.

Goodbye united working class, hello white supremacy!

LOOK IT UP!
Want to know more? Check out the work of historians like Barbara J. Fields, Dr. Nell Painter, and Dr. Edmund Morgan.

1670
Free men of Indigenous and African descent cannot keep Christians as servants.

1680
It becomes illegal for "any negro or other slave" to "raise a HAND to any white person." This strips enslaved people of any right to self-defense, and puts white servants on the same level as the white people who enslave them.

1682
Virginia gives away 50-acre land allotments to "citizens"—and passes a law limiting citizenship to just Europeans.

1691
Anti-miscegenation (interracial marriage) laws are put in place in many states.

1705
Virginia enacts the Slave Codes, a bundle of laws that defined American chattel slavery in its most strict and brutal terms and inspired other colonies to do the same.

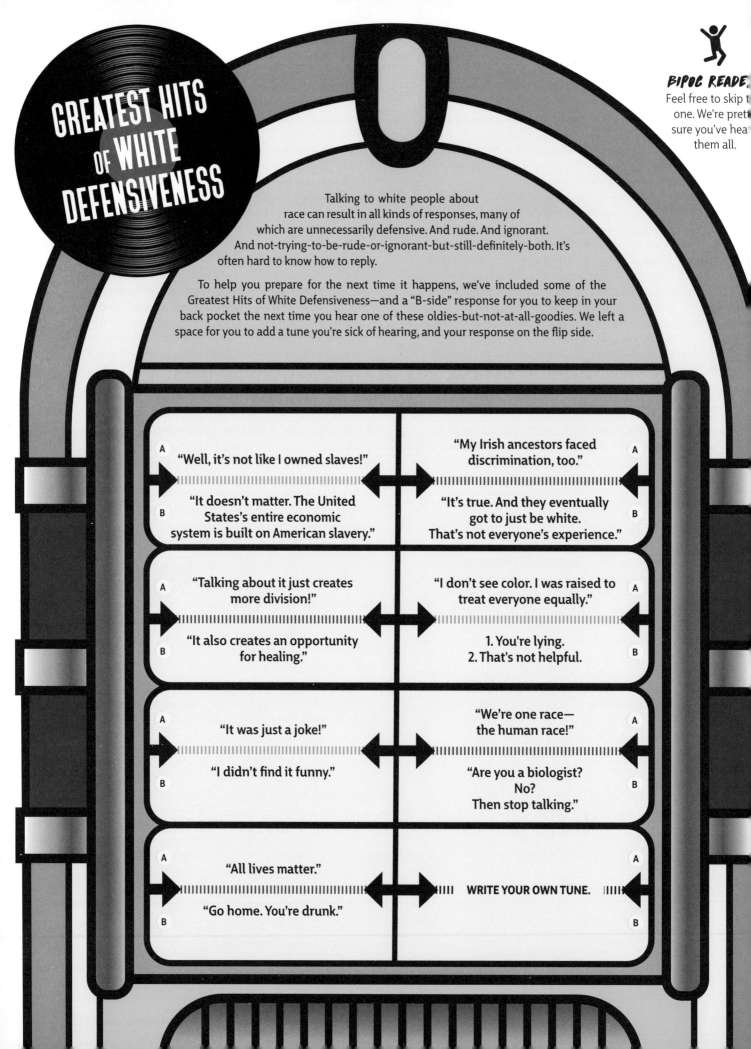

GREATEST HITS OF WHITE DEFENSIVENESS

Talking to white people about race can result in all kinds of responses, many of which are unnecessarily defensive. And rude. And ignorant. And not-trying-to-be-rude-or-ignorant-but-still-definitely-both. It's often hard to know how to reply.

To help you prepare for the next time it happens, we've included some of the Greatest Hits of White Defensiveness—and a "B-side" response for you to keep in your back pocket the next time you hear one of these oldies-but-not-at-all-goodies. We left a space for you to add a tune you're sick of hearing, and your response on the flip side.

A "Well, it's not like I owned slaves!"

B "It doesn't matter. The United States's entire economic system is built on American slavery."

A "My Irish ancestors faced discrimination, too."

B "It's true. And they eventually got to just be white. That's not everyone's experience."

A "Talking about it just creates more division!"

B "It also creates an opportunity for healing."

A "I don't see color. I was raised to treat everyone equally."

B 1. You're lying.
2. That's not helpful.

A "It was just a joke!"

B "I didn't find it funny."

A "We're one race— the human race!"

B "Are you a biologist? No? Then stop talking."

A "All lives matter."

B "Go home. You're drunk."

A WRITE YOUR OWN TUNE.

B

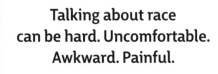

Talking about race can be hard. Uncomfortable. Awkward. Painful.

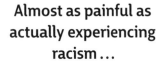

Almost as painful as actually experiencing racism . . .

KS: I'm gonna go ahead and yell that, Kamau. WHITE PEOPLE: IT CAN BE HARD TO TALK ABOUT RACISM. BUT IT'LL NEVER BE AS HARD AS IT IS TO EXPERIENCE RACISM.

WKB: I hope people hear that. Talking about it does often suck—and not just for white people.

KS: Care to elaborate?

WKB: I can only really talk about this from my perspective as a Black man. While some things I experience as a Black American may apply to Latin folks, Asian Americans, and Indigenous people of this land, this is not a one size fits all answer. Also, the experience of a Black woman is very different from that of a Black man. (Thanks, Kimberlé Crenshaw! See pages 56 and 57.) My experience of racism may be analogous to someone else's, but it also may be very different.

KS: Noted.

WKB: But . . . and here's one of the big hurdles in talking to white people about racism. Just because my experience is different than somebody else's, that doesn't necessarily discount the experiences.

KS: Right. Like, "I have never had a negative encounter with the police! I've never heard so-and-so make a racist comment."

WKB: Or this one: "My friend is Black, and that hasn't happened to him."

KS: Which begs the question: If two Black men do the same thing but experience two different outcomes, who do you believe?

WKB: Both. Of. Us.

KS: *GASP*

WKB: Yes, everyone. Two people can go through the same experience and have different results. Like the movie Avatar. I hate it because it's racist. My wife hates it because it's sexist.

KS: I think you're right, actually. But go on.

WKB: One reason it's hard to have discussions about race outside our trusted circles is that they're rarely good faith discussions. White people—and lemme be clear here, this applies to white people of all kinds—don't want to talk about racism. I think it's because honestly discussing race in America challenges their basic assumptions of this country.

KS: Like the whole freedom and democracy and "liberty and justice for all" part.

WKB: Right. And the idea that sure, America has had some problems, but at our core we're a good nation. "We" are good people. Bad things still happen sometimes, but "not in my neighborhood. We're diverse!"

KS: Because if we accept the lie of American exceptionalism, we have to accept the lie of whiteness, and the safety that comes with it. "It can't happen here. It won't happen to me."

WKB: And you can be a Black dude trying to vent about how the supervisor is always commenting on your hair when he doesn't comment on any other coworkers' hair in the office, and then suddenly you're in some weird conversation about how come Black Lives Matter doesn't care about Black-on-Black crime. And—oh, yeah!—YOU'RE THE ONLY BLACK PERSON WHO WORKS IN THIS OFFICE! Add to that just one Ben Carson-y, Candace Owen-y, Kanye West-y, Diamond & Silk-y type of Black person who says something like "Harrumph! I've never experienced racism. I don't know what these other Black people are fussing and fighting about, suh." And the whole conversation is wrecked. It is truly amazing more of us don't . . . what's that thing white people do when they're really mad?

KS: Wear viking costumes and storm the US Capitol?

WKB: I was thinking of "go postal."

But yeah. The challenge of having these conversations is that white people often want to do anything other than have the conversation.

KS: And that's just the first challenge.

WKB: Yup. Then there's the exhaustion. The "I'm too tired today to talk about it" kind, as well as the kind you can only feel when, you know, you and your people and all your descendants have been having the same conversation since those ships, packed to the rafters with enslaved Africans, landed.

KS: It won't shock you to know that I'm not familiar with that level of exhaustion.

WKB: I always imagine those Africans making it through the Middle Passage and thinking, "Welp, it can't get any worse than that boat ride." There is an unbroken line from the unimaginable trauma that those people suffered to what Black Americans experience today.

KS: And you mean that literally—inherited intergenerational trauma is very real.

WKB: Black folks are forever processing racism. That's where we got the Blues, Gospel, R&B, and Hip Hop. But we can't focus on it all the time because we still have to function—gotta pay rent, get a job, deal with racism at our new job, find a newer job, raise our kids in a school system that would prefer they just go to prison, take care of our elders, and our communities, and somehow do all that in a system that uses racism to keep us poor, unhealthy, and undereducated.

KS: I'm listening.

WKB: Then add to that the regularly scheduled news updates featuring Black people like Breonna Taylor, Ahmaud Arbery, Nina Pop, Tony McDade, and Rayshard Brooks who've been murdered by police.

KS: And those are just from 2020.

WKB: Maintaining your well-being can feel like an impossible juggling act. And people of color do it every. Single. Day.

KS: That is depressing.

WKB: PRECISELY. We often try to push the weight of it out of our minds. We don't want to be "the bummer" all the time. We don't want to be the one at the cookout talking about the evils of pork and the importance of managing high blood pressure.

KS: I hear you.

WKB: Thank you for modeling how a white person can just listen and not try to respond with a bunch of their brilliant ideas, like they just discovered the solution to racism!

KS: *[Nods, keeps her mouth shut]*

WKB: It's like talking about gravity. Why be mad at gravity? "This gravity is really preventing me from flying like Superman!" At some point, you get to the place with racism where it's like, "It was like that yesterday. It's like that today. And I'm betting it's going to be like this tomorrow. So **why** are we still acting like it doesn't exist?"

KAREN & KALLIE

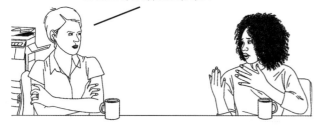

"ARE YOU SURE THAT'S WHAT HAPPENED? IT'S A PRETTY BIG DEAL TO ACCUSE SOMEONE OF SOMETHING LIKE THIS. I'VE WORKED HERE FOR YEARS AND I'VE NEVER NOTICED ANY RACISM AT ALL."

Karen interrupts her colleague and shuts her down by doubting the validity of her experience.

"I HEAR YOU, AND THIS IS NOT OK. I'M SORRY YOU'VE HAD TO DEAL WITH THIS, AND I'M SORRY FOR NOT SEEING IT. THANK YOU FOR TELLING ME."

Kallie listens closely when her colleague approaches her about racism in the workplace. She validates her experience.

COLORING BREAK!

Nina Simone was a brilliant musician and performer as well as a fierce civil rights activist. Put on one of her albums and get inspired and empowered as you color!

How would you define racism? What about white supremacy? Write your answers on the right before reading anything further.

RACISM IS :

How do you feel about your definitions? You feel good? Bad? Racist?

Some people's definitions of racism focus on individual acts of discrimination, like "racism is when a person of one race hates a person of a different race just because of their race." Yes, that's true—but there's much more to it.

Racism is when one group has the power to carry out systematic discrimination by a) the institutional policies and practices of the society, and b) by shaping the cultural beliefs and values that support those racist policies and practices.

In other words, the definition we'll work with is the one taught to us by Black activists, organizers, and community members:

Racism is prejudice plus power.

Prejudice is a fine word for people of different races hating each other. But add *power*—economic, political, cultural, and social—and you have systems that regularly and historically choose one group's hatred over every other group's hatred.

A working definition of **white supremacy is a political and socioeconomic system where white people enjoy structural advantages that other racial and ethnic groups do not.**

WHITE SUPREMACY IS :

SHE DID THE WORK!

In 2020, **Kennedy Mitchum**, a 22-year old Black woman from Florissant, Missouri, got Merriam-Webster—as in, the *literal dictionary*—to revise its definition of "racism" (which hadn't been updated for decades). She was tired of people dismissing her concerns about racism by quoting dictionary definitions that focused on racism as something *individual* rather than *systemic*. So she emailed the Merriam-Webster editors, letting them know that "Racism is not only prejudice against a certain race due to the color of a person's skin, as it states in your dictionary. It is both prejudice combined with social and institutional power. It is a system of advantage based on skin color." She was shocked—and satisfied—when she received a reply the next morning, thanking her for the feedback and committing to updating the definition.

WHITE SUPREMACY WORD SCRAMBLE

To understand white supremacy, we need to understand its history, and work to see all the places it's hiding in plain sight.

DIRECTIONS: Unscramble the terms below, and for a bonus assignment, use FIVE of them in a paragraph about the history of white supremacy in America!

FEDONERATCE AGLF _____

SOTL SECAU _____

KKK _____

PORDU SBYO _____

THIRB FO A NTOINA _____

MIFESTAN TINDESY _____

OLEGNEPYSSI _____

EUNDMD TTPEUS _____

HET GNSSIAP FO TEH GETRA ECRA _____

GUENCISE _____

DRE MMUSRE _____

MEKA AMERICA GTERA NAIGA _____

NSUDWON OWTN _____

Not familiar with these terms? You know what to do! LOOK IT UP!

■ **WRITE YOUR BONUS PARAGRAPH HERE** ■

```
Q U Q Y R X Z O C M N J A M I S S J I Z
I Z Z E C D T E E E L E N N D S Y Z K P
H N W I D A H I C K H N T U M E S R C K
P O S S L I M I W H T E I A J N T D V R
P R L T S T D E Q F R A B L Z E E K Z R
B O I T I U C N R P O N L L K T M Z J U
A I O V J T E A E P V H A Y Y I I H B E
W R A E I B U R P J U S C Z U H C I O L
Y R R S Z L S T A M J S K H D W T U I A
H P R A R O E L I D I H N N I D J E Y M
E Z L B N A V G A O L X E H B I P O C U
L V X A H W M M E H N R S V P T K O O A
M J L R T R S Y Z Y O A S V L O U B A R
E C I L P M O C C A C M L T N E T N I T
D E F E N S I V E F M J E X E F Z Q Z E
H Q K T F F Z M A B W W Y A U V F C E C
G N N H F J B S V B R Y G O X G O J O K
B C C Y D B U H H L P K I E V S B S M Y
D I S C R I M I N A T I O N S P L U K H
J D A P H F X A A J Q K G Q A Z Q F H O
```

 **WORD SEARCH**

Hidden in this scramble are terms and concepts that we cover in the book. Keep an eye out for them as you read—and circle them in the scramble above.

ACCOMPLICE   HISTORY   PRIVILEGE
ALLY   IMPACT   SUPREMACY
ANTIBLACKNESS   INSTITUTIONAL   SYSTEMIC
BIAS   INTENT   TRAUMA
BIPOC   INTERPERSONAL   WHITENESS
DEFENSIVE   POWER
DISCRIMINATION   PREJUDICE   Answers on page 153

LET'S DEFINE SOME KEY TERMS!

DIRECTIONS: Match the terms below to the definitions.

___ Antiblackness   ___ Individual Racism

___ Bias   ___ Institutional Racism

___ Discrimination   ___ Internalized Racism

___ Equality   ___ Prejudice

___ Equity   ___ Privilege

___ Impact   ___ Structural Racism

___ Intent

1 A preconceived judgment about a person or group of people, usually indicating negative bias. (Also, really hard to spell.)

2 The beliefs, attitudes, and actions of individuals that support or perpetuate racism in conscious and unconscious ways.

3 Racist policies and practices that give unfair advantages to white people over people of color. These policies often never mention any racial group, but the intent is to create disparity.

4 A state of fairness in which everyone has what they need in order to achieve that goal.

5 The social advantages granted to and experienced by members of dominant groups at the expense of members of nondominant groups.

6 The private racial beliefs held by and within individuals, usually absorbed via social, familial, political, and religious messages about race.

7 The desired result of your words, actions, and efforts.

8 The overarching system of racial bias across institutions and society that systematically privilege white people and disadvantage people of color.

9 A disproportionate weight in favor of or against an idea or a thing.

10 The actual result of your words, actions, and efforts.

11 The unjust or prejudicial treatment of different categories of people or things, especially on the grounds of race, age, or sex. In other words: prejudice + action.

12 A state of fairness in which everyone has the same amount, despite their existing needs or assets.

13 The specific kinds of discrimination faced by Black individuals.

Answers on page 153

SPOT THE RACIST BS

WKB: A big part of understanding race and racism in America is paying attention to how race is presented, discussed, and produced all around you.

KS: Racism is especially insidious and sneaky. It constantly shows up from companies or organizations or people we expect to "do better."

WKB: You might call this stuff "subtle"—but it doesn't feel subtle when I notice it. You might call these "microaggressions," but honestly? Can we just drop the "micro"? That makes it sound almost cute. Death by a thousand papercuts is still pretty damn aggressive. **A microaggression is just racism that didn't get me killed.**

KS: Let's practice your racist-bullshit-spotting skills. We'll start with the back of a box of Corn Pops. For real.

WKB: Below is an actual image from the back of an actual box of Corn Pops that ended up going viral because it's . . . actually pretty racist. Do you see it?

Well?! Did you spot the ONE BROWN CORN POP who's cleaning up while all the other same-colored yellow corn pops are having the time of their corn-popping lives?! And this cereal is marketed to children, many of whom know what it's like to be the only brown corn pop in a sea of yellow ones. Children all over the country, getting a side of racist bullshit with their morning serving of high-fructose corn syrup.

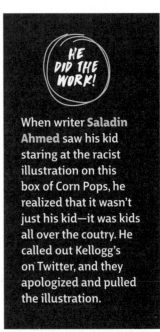

HE DID THE WORK!

When writer **Saladin Ahmed** saw his kid staring at the racist illustration on this box of Corn Pops, he realized that it wasn't just his kid—it was kids all over the coutry. He called out Kellogg's on Twitter, and they apologized and pulled the illustration.

DIRECTIONS: Look closely at each image, and CIRCLE THE RACIST BULLSHIT!

Here's a nice poster about swimming pool safety that the Red Cross made in 2014. The kids and adults who are following the rules are "cool." Anyone who misbehaves is "uncool." Notice anything wrong?

Here's a brochure from 2015, for a Continuing Education program at the University of North Georgia. It aims to recruit students for a Leadership Training program. How does this look to you?

Most of the "uncool" people present as BIPOC!

A Black boy is leading a white boy down the primrose path of bad behavior!

The one white-presenting person marked as "uncool" on their own is the kid carrying a bottle. The way this poster is going, I'm just gonna assume he's a light-skinned Latino teenager.

Also what is that whale doing? Whales can't fly.

Oh hey! All the "cool" people present as white!

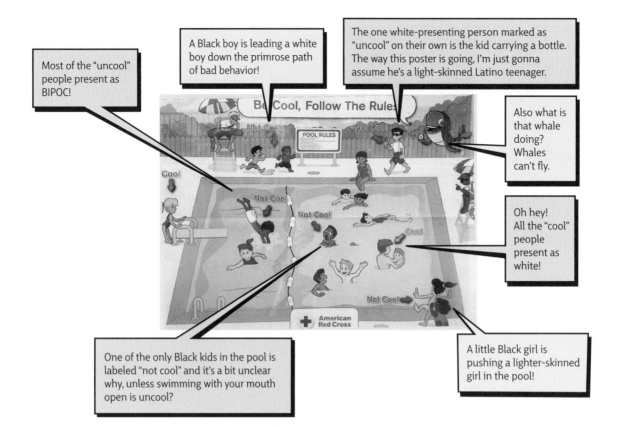

One of the only Black kids in the pool is labeled "not cool" and it's a bit unclear why, unless swimming with your mouth open is uncool?

A little Black girl is pushing a lighter-skinned girl in the pool!

The Black man is running so hard he's about to fall. Is his hand tied behind his back? Are they making him do this one-handed?

What does CE stand for? Caucasian Excellence?

White woman's working hard, but the white dudes are still ahead. She's maybe 81 percent of the way there? Get it? Because the wage gap? Because white women in America make 81 cents to the dollar that white men make? And Black women make 63 cents to the dollar—so maybe there's actually a Black woman in this race, but we can't see her, because she's so damn far back!

While the Black man stumbles, the white dude on the right is super calm, like a white Usain Bolt coasting across the finish line. Let's be honest here—how many times have you seen white guys beating Black guys in races? (WKB: I wrote this one, everyone, so it's OK.)

And she's wearing high heels. In a foot race.

Cool slogan: "Why follow when you can lead?" Yet, who is following— and who is leading?

The white guy who has "won" the race looks pretty happy—for himself. No glance back to check on or help his opponents. Is that how we're teaching "leadership" these days?

The University of North Georgia is a PWI (a predominantly white institution) with a white population of more than 50 percent. The Black student body is less than 5 percent Cool cool cool.

WHITE SUPREMACY ICEBERG

When we say that something is "just the tip of the iceberg" we mean the thing we actually know about is just a fraction of what's really there. About 90 percent of an iceberg exists below the surface—we only see the top of it.

Think of white supremacy as an iceberg: The icy part sticking out of the sea gets the headlines. The over-the-top racism that gets us all nodding in agreement. (Well, most of us.)

But beneath the surface is where most of white supremacy's damage is done. The further below the surface you go, the harder it can be to identify the white supremacy-ness of an action or a person. But that doesn't make it any less harmful or insidious.

Each one of these levels is maintained by people who are active and complicit (mainly by staying quiet and pretending it doesn't exist).

DIRECTIONS:

1 **Read** the examples.

2 **Draw a line** to connect the examples to where you think they belong on the iceberg.

3 **There are no right or wrong answers**—your sense of what's visible and what's hidden will depend on who you are, where you live, and your life experience.

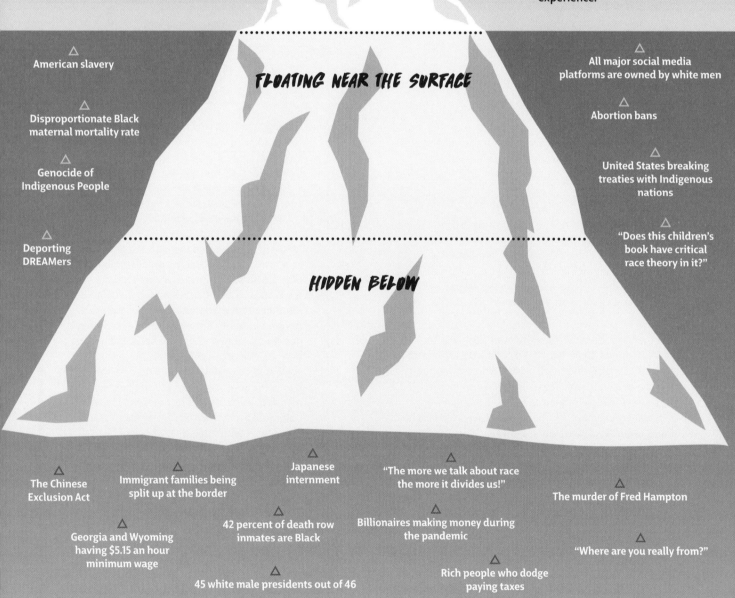

OVER THE TOP

FLOATING NEAR THE SURFACE

HIDDEN BELOW

American slavery

Disproportionate Black maternal mortality rate

Genocide of Indigenous People

Deporting DREAMers

All major social media platforms are owned by white men

Abortion bans

United States breaking treaties with Indigenous nations

"Does this children's book have critical race theory in it?"

The Chinese Exclusion Act

Immigrant families being split up at the border

Japanese internment

"The more we talk about race the more it divides us!"

The murder of Fred Hampton

Georgia and Wyoming having $5.15 an hour minimum wage

42 percent of death row inmates are Black

Billionaires making money during the pandemic

"Where are you really from?"

45 white male presidents out of 46

Rich people who dodge paying taxes

Mass incarceration

American Indian reservations have higher poverty levels

Your "NAMAslay" yoga tank-top

Islamophobia

So now we understand racism, right? Let's talk about antiracism.

ANTIRACISM IS :

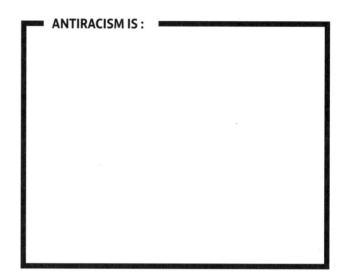

WKB: Here's how Dr. Ibram X. Kendi breaks it down in his book *How to Be an Antiracist*:

> **RACIST:** One who is supporting a racist policy through their actions or inaction or expressing a racist idea.

> **ANTIRACIST:** One who is supporting an antiracist policy through their actions or expressing an antiracist idea.

Antiracism begins with accepting and admitting your own racism. And being really damn self-aware.

KS: Whew. Exhausting, right? Almost as exhausting as . . .

WKB: ACTUALLY LIVING WITH RAAAAAAAACISM!

KS: Being *antiracist* is not the same thing as being *not racist*. The vast majority of people likely consider themselves "not racist." Even white supremacists are notorious for saying they're "not racist." This nation's history is littered with explanations and excuses that cover up and cloak plain old nasty racism like . . . well, like hoods.

WKB: As Dr. Crystal M. Fleming put it in her book *How to Be Less Stupid About Race*: "White supremacy continues to persist, in part, due to the widespread temptation to only see and *condemn other people's racism*—racism is always somebody else's crime."

Not doing anything isn't being "not racist." When it comes to justice, there's no in-between. There *aren't* "good people on both sides."

KS: WE WANT YOU TO BE ANTIRACIST. That is the goal.

WKB: To be clear, it's not a one-time achievement. You're not gonna just check "Become an antiracist" off your to-do list. It's an ongoing process, and you're ideally raising the stakes for yourself, always striving to be better.

DO THE READING

Not doing anything isn't being "not racist." When it comes to justice, there's no in-between. There aren't "good people on both sides."

The "moderate" is racist, too. And you know who had something to say about the danger of being a moderate? Dr. Martin Luther King Jr., who wrote in his "Letter From Birmingham Jail":

> *I have almost reached the regrettable conclusion that the Negro's great stumbling block in his stride toward freedom is not the White Citizen's Council-er or the Ku Klux Klanner, but the white moderate who is more devoted to "order" than to justice; who prefers a negative peace which is the absence of tension to a positive peace which is the presence of justice; who constantly says "I agree with you in the goal you seek, but I can't agree with your methods of direct action . . ." who paternalistically feels he can set the timetable for another man's freedom; who lives by a mythical concept of time and who constantly advises the Negro to wait for a "more convenient season.*

- "Letter From Birmingham Jail" by Dr. Martin Luther King Jr.

- *How To Be Less Stupid About Race* by Crystal M. Fleming

- *How To Be An Antiracist* by Ibram X. Kendi

YOU MIGHT BE AN ANTIRACIST IF...

DIRECTIONS: CHECK the ☐ if the statement already applies to you—
and be honest! CHECK the ○ if you aspire to it.

☐ ○ You know beyond a shadow of a doubt that the United States of America values white lives over all other lives. (For people of color, accepting this is not much of a stretch. But for many white people, this can be a pretty big deal.)

☐ ○ You know that you have internalized racism—and you will work to unlearn and reject it.

☐ ○ You know that the United States was built on, and still benefits from, two war crimes: the genocide of the Indigenous tribes and the transatlantic slave trade.

☐ ○ You understand that your actions and behaviors matter way more than what you say, post, or plaster on the bumper of your car.

☐ ○ You notice racist behavior in your workplace/school/church/neighborhood/family and speak up, rather than waiting for a BIPOC person to bring it up.

☐ ○ You give a shit about how people of color are treated in this country and your community.

☐ ○ You know that institutional buddy systems of legacy admission to colleges and universities, white fraternities and sororities, country clubs, "secret societies," chambers of commerce, golf courses, and rotary clubs have historically allowed white people to assemble among themselves and guarantee that even the most mediocre of them could achieve great success.

☐ ○ You don't feel the need to declare "I'm not racist!" because you know that literally every person who does some racist bullshit says that.

☐ ○ You don't say things like, "I like all kinds of music ... except rap!"

☐ ○ You ask to speak to the manager because you witness something shitty happening to *someone else*, not just to you.

☐ ○ You read books by people of color even when it's not February.

☐ ○ You observe how policies and systems in your community uphold white supremacy and a) actively resist them, and b) actively support new policies and systems that lead to racial justice.

☐ ○ You work to make sure you are pronouncing people's names the way they want them pronounced.

☐ ○ You don't ask to touch the hair of someone that you aren't parenting or in an intimate relationship with unless their hair is on fire and you have a bucket of water.

☐ ○ You bring up racial justice when everything is "normal" and "fine"—not just when it's in the news.

☐ ○ You listen to ideas from BIPOC thinkers and activists, even the ones that feel outside your ideological comfort zone.

☐ ○ You know that affirmative action is an effort to take white supremacy's pasty thumb off the scales so Black people can get a more fair shot at life. And you know that affirmative action is not an effort to pass over more qualified white people.

☐ ○ You're OK with the fact that it's just not about you!

☐ ○ You accept that you'll get it wrong—and you work on not freezing up or crumbling into an ashamed mess when it happens.

☐ ○ You listen when people of color share their experiences with white supremacy and respond in a way that validates their experiences, rather than centering your own.

☐ ○ You're not perfect, but you're trying. On a pretty regular basis. You're curious. You're tired and overwhelmed. You're committed.

"FRUITS OF ONE'S LABOR" By Adesina O. Koiki

This puzzle is inspired by a professional baseball player who changed the game forever in 1969 when he refused a trade, told the Commissioner of Baseball "I do not regard myself as a piece of property to be bought or sold," and sued Major League Baseball for his professional freedom. While he lost the lawsuit against MLB (and his playing career), his bold actions ushered in the "free agent" revolution in baseball.

ACROSS

1 Early app version
5 Head honcho
9 An uncomfortable thing in one's throat, metaphorically
10 It's often found in geometry class
11 With 4-Down, what 15-Across fought to become after refusing a trade in 1969
12 Debate squad
13 Something "picked" by a pedant
15 Athlete who fought indentured servitude in Major League Baseball
21 ___-Wan Kenobi (Star Wars sage)
22 Guy
23 Raid, for example
25 ___ Clause (contract stipulation that gave teams the right to trade and sell players without their consent, abolished by MLB in 1975)
26 Overly inquisitive person

DOWN

1 Lifelong pal, in textspeak
2 Provide work for fact-checkers, say
3 Hammer ___ (crooked digit)
4 See 11-Across
5 Call for action?
6 Material in a mother lode
7 Realm of Poseidon, Neptune, and Yemaya
8 Soul singer Cooke
14 Not as certain

15 Many a character on *Hill Street Blues*
16 Car ordered on the phone
17 Maya Angelou's "And Still I ___"
18 Shade of green
19 Venus, vis-à-vis Serena
20 Actor Daniel-___ Kim
24 Recipe amount: Abbr.

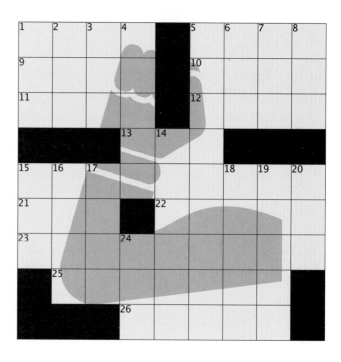

Answers on page 156

MY ANTIRACISM CONTRACT

On _____
[TODAY'S DATE]

I, _____ , aka _____ , am a(n) _____ . Officially, I am
[YOUR GOVERNMENT NAME]   [THE NAME THAT YOUR CLOSE FRIENDS CALL YOU]   [NATIONALITY]

racially _____ . And I see myself as _____ ,
[THE RACE BOX YOU CHECK ON GOVERNMENT FORMS]   [WORD(S) YOU USE TO DEFINE YOUR RACE]

_____ , _____ . I hereby acknowledge that racism is _____ ,
[OTHER WORD THAT DEFINES YOU]   [OTHER WORD THAT DEFINES YOU]   [WORD OF CERTITUDE]

and that the United States of America was founded on a system of white supremacy by privileged,

Christian, white _____ men.
[AD HOMINEM ATTACK]

And while certainly no white person who is currently living (not even _____)
[NAME OF VERY, VERY OLD FAMOUS WHITE PERSON]

owned enslaved Africans, I acknowledge, accept, _____ that every white person who is
[FUN VERB THAT MEANS "I GET IT"]

currently living, including _____ , benefits from that system of white
[NAME OF A FAMOUS YOUNG WHITE PERSON WHO SEEMS PRETTY COOL]

supremacy. And I also want to acknowledge that seeing all of that written out in the previous sentence

makes me feel _____ .
[FEELING WORD]

America has done a(n) _____ job of atoning for or even acknowledging its original twin crimes
[ADJECTIVE]

of chattel slavery and Indigenous genocide (including what was done to _____).
[PEOPLE INDIGENOUS TO WHERE YOU LIVE]

I personally have done a(n) _____ job of acknowledging this, and confronting how
[PERSONALLY RELEVANT ADJECTIVE]

white supremacy functions within me. In my personal life, I experience racism _____ ,
[WORD OF REGULARITY]

and I know I can do a _____ job of confronting it. There are specific areas where I'm just
[MODIFIER]

really _____ when it comes to dealing with racism, including _____ . Sometimes
[ADJECTIVE]   [AREA]

when it comes to actively being an antiracist, I'm like _____ when
[FAMOUS PERSON YOU DON'T LIKE]

they _____ but they wish they were _____ .
[INSERT ACTIVITY YOU HATE THAT THEY DO]   [NAME OF YOUR FAVORITE SUPER SMART PERSON]

When it comes to being an antiracist, I accept that I won't get it right 100 percent of the time, and I will

probably _____ approximately _____ percent of the time, but I will keep doing
[SYNONYM FOR MESS UP, BUT MORE CREATIVE]   [NUMBER]

the work. And not just by myself! I'm going to use what I learn in this book to finally get through

to _____ . And I'm finally going to read _____
[PERSON IN YOUR LIFE WHO ALSO NEEDS TO DO THE WORK]   [BOOK ON RACISM THAT YOU HAVE ALWAYS TOLD YOURSELF THAT YOU

_____ . And when I'm done I'm going to be just as cool as _____ .
SHOULD READ BUT HAVE NEVER READ]   [INSERT YOUR ANTIRACIST HERO]

I am _____ , and I am a practicing antiracist.
[YOUR NAME]

CHAPTER 2

It's My Privilege

WHEN SQUARING UP against a challenge like dismantling white supremacy, it helps to know what resources you have at your disposal. Turns out, your privileges are some of your best resources. In this chapter we'll:

➡️ Define privilege, identify our privileges, and move through the prickly resistance that might pop up.

➡️ Clarify related concepts like intersectionality.

➡️ Debunk the myth of "bootstrapping" via a board game.

➡️ Make a detailed plan for leveraging your privileges to dismantle white supremacy.

SUPPLIES

SCISSORS

SINGLE DIE

INTERNET

PARTNER

PEN/PENCIL

ART SUPPLIES

I would like to start this chapter by acknowledging something important about privilege: It's hard to spell. I still mess it up all the time.

I can spell pretty well. It is one of my privileges.

WKB: Why do you think such a basic idea makes so many white folks—well meaning and otherwise—turn into colicky babies?

KS: That's unfair to colicky babies. They can't help it.

WKB: True. Sorry, babies.

KS: But you're right, a lot of grown-ass adults really lose their shit at the mere mention of "white privilege." Like, all-defenses-activated! We turn into guilty, defensive, awkward armadillos? Is this the right animal metaphor?

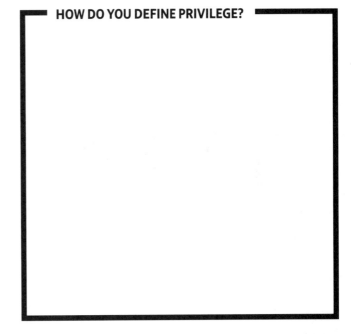

WKB: *[Googles "armadillo reaction"]* "When threatened, the armadillo will curl up into a ball."

KS: YES! Some white people feel all messed up about the fact that we have something about us that makes our lives easier and we don't really feel it. It just is. And we don't like the fact that we don't feel it. We feel like . . .

WKB: Like normal people. You're just a normal person.

KS: Yup. As shitty as it is to admit, "white privilege" is what most white Americans define as just being a person. And when we hear "white privilege" we suddenly have to think about our whiteness—our race—as "a thing."

WKB: Wow. What's that like?

KS: It's not easy. It can be destabilizing. And it often involves a lot of cognitive dissonance.

WKB: *[Sigh]*

KS: We like this common definition of privilege: *Unearned access to social power accorded by the formal and informal institutions of society to ALL members of a dominant group.*

HOW DO YOU DEFINE PRIVILEGE?

And in fact, most of us have some form of unearned social privilege. Most of have been granted unearned social rewards and access to power because of our race, gender, sexuality, class status, etc.

WKB: We all have levels of privilege that aren't race-based, but when combined with our racial categorization can either help close the gap or widen the gap. Depending which side of the gap you're on.

KS: For example . . .

WKB: A Black kid is born in Brooklyn in the early '60s. His family moves him to North Carolina. Again, this is in the early '60s, so however bad racism was in Brooklyn then,

WITHOUT THINKING TOO MUCH ABOUT IT, WRITE DOWN FOUR OF YOUR PRIVILEGES RIGHT NOW:

1

2

3

4

How was it?
Was it hard?
Was it fun?
Are you an
armadillo now?

Your
face
here?!

control how hard he worked, he didn't control how tall he was. At least I don't think he could. But George W. Bush C-minused his way through life all the way to the freaking presidency. Even though by some accounts all he wanted was to be the Commissioner of Baseball. That's white privilege. Literally NO Black, Indigenous, Latino/a, or Asian American person can accidentally end up the president. Barack Obama did it against all odds. George W. Bush did it with all the odds in his favor: white, rich, Ivy League, dad also was a president. Plus a wife willing to put up with his nonsense. AND HE STILL NEEDED THE SUPREME COURT TO WIN THE ELECTION FOR HIM! I'm sorry. I'm getting worked up.

KS: No problem. What you're pointing out is that (drum roll) MULTIPLE TRUTHS CAN COEXIST! AT THE SAME TIME! You can simultaneously belong to a privileged dominant group and a nondominant group. In fact, that's the case for most of us (who aren't straight and rich cis white dudes).

WKB: And that often seems to be the core of the armadillo freak-out: White people are like, "But I worked hard! You don't know my life! I haven't had privileges!"

KS: No one wants to think they have a leg up on others for "no reason." Acknowledging my privilege doesn't mean I haven't worked super hard to get to where I am (I have) or that I haven't struggled or suffered (to be honest, I really haven't, but still). It means that I've been able to move through the world receiving support and assistance—often unacknowledged—because of my whiteness. Not having to think about my whiteness is the biggest privilege there is.

I'd rather grow up there than North Carolina. But for some reason that kid happens to have a manically competitive spirit and is a head taller than anybody in his family. His name is **Michael Jordan.**

KS: I get it. Do another one.

WKB: A white kid is born in Connecticut in the mid-1940s. He is born into an accomplished, successful family, but by all accounts is kind of a goofball. Not great in school. Has an unspectacular career in the military. Has a substance abuse problem. Has a brother who's the star of the family who he can't ever hope to live up to. He ends up being . . .

KS: GEORGE W. BUSH!

WKB: Yup! Michael Jordan was born Black into a racist world but was able to work his way out of it, but while he could

DO THE READING

Learn more about whiteness and privilege by reading:

• "Black Reconstruction" an essay by W. E. B Du Bois, written in 1935

• "White Privilege: Unpacking the Invisible Knapsack" by Peggy McIntosh. Be sure to read Prof. McIntosh's notes for facilitators, which can be found online at the National SEED Project. This is a great group activity, so consider reading it with friends.

TO ACKNOWLEDGE PRIVILEGE is the FIRST STEP in MAKING IT AVAILABLE FOR WIDER USE

—AUDRE LORDE

COLORING BREAK!

The great writer, poet, and visionary Audre Lorde wrote this in her journal on December 15, 1986; it was published in *A Burst of Light*.

CHECK YOUR PRIVILEGE

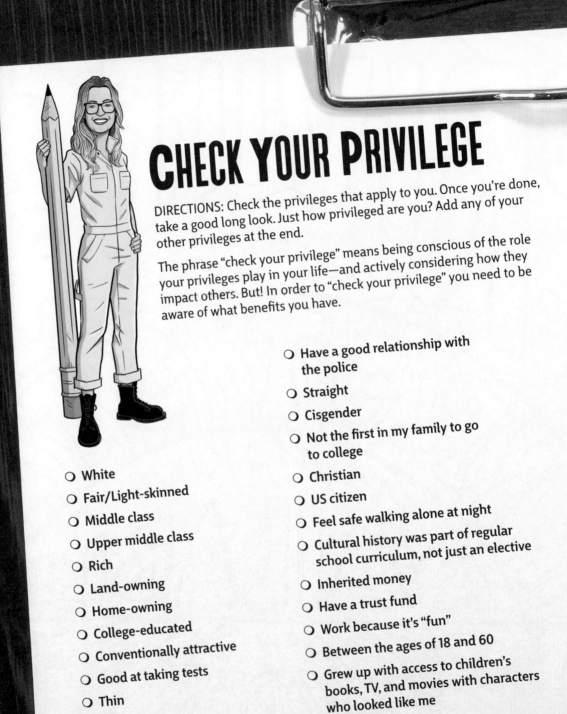

DIRECTIONS: Check the privileges that apply to you. Once you're done, take a good long look. Just how privileged are you? Add any of your other privileges at the end.

The phrase "check your privilege" means being conscious of the role your privileges play in your life—and actively considering how they impact others. But! In order to "check your privilege" you need to be aware of what benefits you have.

- ○ White
- ○ Fair/Light-skinned
- ○ Middle class
- ○ Upper middle class
- ○ Rich
- ○ Land-owning
- ○ Home-owning
- ○ College-educated
- ○ Conventionally attractive
- ○ Good at taking tests
- ○ Thin
- ○ Tall
- ○ Thick in the "right" places
- ○ Hearing
- ○ Seeing
- ○ Live in a "safe" neighborhood
- ○ Debt-free
- ○ Nondisabled

- ○ Have a good relationship with the police
- ○ Straight
- ○ Cisgender
- ○ Not the first in my family to go to college
- ○ Christian
- ○ US citizen
- ○ Feel safe walking alone at night
- ○ Cultural history was part of regular school curriculum, not just an elective
- ○ Inherited money
- ○ Have a trust fund
- ○ Work because it's "fun"
- ○ Between the ages of 18 and 60
- ○ Grew up with access to children's books, TV, and movies with characters who looked like me
- ○ Neurotypical
- ○ Not worried about being threatened, harassed, or harmed because of my identity
- ○ Reading this in my first language
- ○ Tall
- ○ A cis man

- ○ Have health insurance
- ○ Housed
- ○ Employed
- ○ Married
- ○ Blue-eyed
- ○ Green-eyed
- ○ Have an "American" sounding name
- ○ Blond-haired
- ○ No speech impediment
- ○ Full head of hair
- ○ Athletic
- ○ Good teeth
- ○ Can pay rent every month
- ○ Always able to pay utility bills
- ○ Never been in prison
- ○ Laugh easily
- ○ Not worried about money
- ○ Have "connections" with "friends in high places"
- ○ Understand the stock market
- ○ Often put in charge of things
- ○ Everybody in my home has their own room
- ○ Have a well-worn passport
- ○ Have employees
- ○ Are an actual billionaire
- ○ Regularly fly first class
- ○ Get doctor appointments easily
- ○ Have time for hobbies and leisure
- ○ Aren't afraid of a medical bill
- ○ Clothes sold in stores fit my body
- ○ Regularly get a good night's sleep
- ○ Are or have been the president of the United States
- ○ Have gotten away with yelling at a cop
- ○ Own a professional sports team
- ○ Am George Clooney
- ○ Right-handed
- ○ Parents are alive, married, and nice to me
- ○ Get invited to cool parties
- ○ Car registration is paid
- ○ Are offended by the term "Karen"
- ○ Feel mildly annoyed by parking tickets
- ○ Took a selfie with a cop while storming the US Capitol
- ○ Own multiple functioning cars
- ○ Not afraid to show ID
- ○ Can easily access buildings I need to go into
- ○ Know how to swim
- ○ Was invited to Obama's 60th birthday party
- ○ Think Bill Maher is funny
- ○ Understand memes
- ○ Have a strong Wi-Fi connection
- ○ Can easily access fresh food
- ○ Not kept up at night by the sounds of sirens and gunshots
- ○ Not worried about family members getting deported
- ○ Friends and family share my belief systems
- ○
- ○
- ○

PORTRAITS OF PRIVILEGE

DIRECTIONS: Make your privileges visible by drawing them in the frame below. Feel free to be abstract!

Unearned social privileges can be hard to identify because we're taught not to see them as privileges—we might see them as things we earned or are entitled to, or as just kind of "the way things are." Also, many privileges aren't phenotypical: things like good health, a neurotypical brain, and a big ol' trust fund aren't always visible to others.

This exercise might be helpful if thinking about your privilege feels icky, shameful, or uncomfortable. Art can be a good way to express things that we aren't yet comfortable talking about.

 ## COLORING BREAK!

The Atlanta Dream players have done the work many times, leveraging their privilege as highly visible (yet underpaid*) professional athletes to take strong stands in support of racial justice—and to oppose censorship by a team owner. In 2020, Atlanta Dream co-owner Kelly Loeffler, a white conservative state Senator, demanded that the team stop wearing "Black Lives Matter" shirts during games. In response, the team debuted new T-shirts during a televised game. They read "Vote Warnock," a reference to Loeffler's Senate opponent, Raphael Warnock. Photos of the players went viral, and the Dream is credited with raising awareness of Warnock's campaign. He went on to beat Loeffler in a runoff election, becoming the first Black Democrat elected to the Senate from the South— and helping Democrats secure control of the Senate.

*WNBA players make $1 for every $7 that their male NBA counterparts. Players are doing the work to organize and demand pay equity in their league, and for women in all fields.

KS: Wow. I basically checked off every single box except for "I'm a billionaire" and "I'm George Clooney," which you clearly snuck in there, Kamau.

WKB: And how do you feel now?

KS: [*Turns into an armadillo*]

WKB: Dude, for real?

KS: Just kidding! MY NAME IS KATE AND I'M PRIVILEGED AF! I'm a fourth-generation homeowner on stolen land, in one of the most expensive real estate markets in the country. I'm descended from Europeans who chose to come to this country. I'm descended from enslavers and Confederate soldiers. I was raised in a two-parent middle-class household on an all-white block in a "safe" neighborhood. I didn't experience a workplace that wasn't predominantly white until I was in my midtwenties—and it was incredibly eye-opening. My parents paid for my undergraduate education and I only had a small amount of student debt from my Ivy League master's degree, which I've paid off. I DRIVE A NEW VOLVO SUV (and I complain about how the touch screen interface is "really annoying").

WKB: It's a privilege to even talk about my privileges! I'm 6'4" and physically strong, which means I can get things off a high shelf, carry my kids, help my friends move (though I'd prefer not to), and literally stand up and over

people who are being jerks. In recent years, I've been paid well enough to buy a house in a neighborhood I feel safe in, go on vacations, and take care of multiple generations of my family. Despite being a college dropout, I am well educated. I'm tech-savvy and a quick learner, and I am not intimidated by new ideas like Tik Tok dances, vaccines, or toys that need too many batteries. I'm heterosexual and never had to worry whether I'd be allowed to get married. And thanks to Richard and Mildred Loving, I was allowed to marry my white wife. Also, because I've gone to private schools, lived and traveled all over the country, and been in a relationship with a white woman, I know how to be around all types of white people (from corporate whites to nice liberals to KKK members). And that's a necessary survival tool in this country.

KS: Honestly, it's all pretty simple and straightforward.

WKB: Yet people reallllly lose their shit when they hear the word.

KS: Should we say it again, just to piss more people off?

WKB: YOU HAVE PRIVILEEEEEEEEEEGE!!!

REMINDER!

Some privilege categories are fixed, while others can shift over time. If you're a gainfully employed homeowner, we hope you can stay that way— but that's not always the case.

REMINDER!

Acknowledging privilege isn't a burden—it's an opportunity to learn and be better, so we can work toward a more just and inclusive world.

REMINDER!

You're not a bad person if you benefit from privilege. But you ain't shit if you don't do anything with it.

KAREN & KALLIE

KAREN gets upset when her friend mentions privilege.

KALLIE thinks critically about her own privilege and is willing to have an honest conversation about it.

PRIVILEGE BY THE NUMBERS

Unearned social privileges have real-world consequences.

DIRECTIONS: Read the statistics below. Pick ONE fact to learn more about, then work it into a conversation with someone.

36 percent of white job applicants receive more **callbacks** than Black applicants and 24 percent receive more than Latino/a applicants.

In a study on weight-based discrimination, **60 percent of participants reported experiencing weight/height discrimination** that interferes with their employment on average four times during their life.

Asian and Black job applicants are more than twice as likely to be called for an interview if they whitewash their résumés by changing their name and excluding cultural accolades.

Black women who have natural hair (including Afros, twists, and braids) are often perceived as less professional than Black women with straightened hair, and white women with a variety of hairstyles.

Elderly lesbian couples **receive 15 percent less in social security** benefits than straight couples.

21 percent of transgender, genderqueer, and gender-expansive college students have **reported being sexually assaulted**.

Laws targeting unhoused people (including criminalizing lying down in public) **have increased in cities by 119 percent since 2011.**

A young adult's **likelihood of being a homeowner increases 8.4 percentage points** if their parents are homeowners.

Though more than 15 percent of households in the United States are home to someone with a physical disability, **only 6 percent of homes are designed with physical accessibility in mind.**

$10,000

AAPI and Latinx trans people are six times more likely than their cis counterparts to have a yearly annual income below $10,000.

Indigenous women are **twice as likely than women of any other race to experience rape or sexual assault**.

Black people are more often diagnosed with schizophrenia and less frequently diagnosed with mood disorders than white people with the same symptoms. They are offered medication or therapy at lower rates than the **general population.**

*Indigenous children and adolescents in the United States have **the highest rates of self-reported depression** than any other ethnic or racial group in the country.*

GRATEFUL

INCRIMINATED

NAUSEOUS

PROUD

CONFUSED

MEH

FINE

GUILTY

WORRIED

I CHECKED MY PRIVILEGE(S) AND NOW I FEEL:

DIRECTIONS: Circle all that apply!

VALIDATED

CURIOUS

SHITTY

EMBARRASSED

GREAT

RELIEVED

YOUR REACTIONS ARE your own. They're valid, and they're real. The more you allow yourself to be held back by shame and guilt, the more you disempower yourself and your potential for action. Get out of your own way so you can make shit happen!

ASHAMED

"I was today years old when I realized that _____ is actually a form of unearned social privilege."

🎲 BOOTSTRAPPING: THE GAME!

"Bootstrapping" is the classic American myth that every hardworking individual should be able to pull themselves up by their bootstraps and succeed, with no help from anyone, and no "handouts" from the government! All you need to do is believe in yourself and work hard, and you'll get what you deserve. Right?! Anyone who doesn't succeed? They're not trying hard enough. They're lazy.

This is also known as "the myth of meritocracy."

Here's the thing: To pull yourself up by your bootstraps you need to have a pair of boots to begin with. You need to have access to boots, the funds to buy them, and an understanding of how to walk in them. The reality is, the path to success doesn't look the same for everyone....

DIRECTIONS:

⇨ **YOU'LL NEED** 2 players, a pair of scissors, and a single die.

⇨ **CUT OUT YOUR GAME PIECES**, located in the lower left corner.

⇨ **CHOOSE YOUR LANE:** Play as A White Man or The Other.

⇨ **ROLL THE DIE** and follow the instructions on the squares.

⇨ **FIRST PERSON** to get to the FINISH wins!

Hear interesting story about boots on NPR.

"These boots will look great with that jacket."

Get a raise at work! Plan to buy the limited edition boots.

"Here, take this complimentary pair of cashmere socks."

"Hi! Welcome to the Boot Store! How can we help you?"

CONGRATS! YOU GOT YOUR BOOTS! Pull yourself up by those shiny new straps and move on up!

"Hey man, nice boots!"

You did it! You've achieved the American Dream!

Boot store is in an "up-and-coming" neighborhood. Tell your friends you discovered it.

Feel guilty for 10 seconds that boots are made with child labor.

Come up with an idea for an app that replaces the need for boots. Get investor funding and go straight to the Finish!

Boot store is not wheelchair accessible. Skip 2 turns while they finally comply with ADA regulations.

Call boot store to confirm their hours and location. When the owner hears your accent, he hangs up.

"What country are you from, anyway?"

Get pulled over for broken tail light. Move back 3 spaces.

"Do you have to be so loud?"

Boot store is blocked by people protesting unfair labor practices. Join them, but miss a turn.

"Hello? Does anyone work here? I've been waiting for 20 minutes... I'd like to buy some boots please?" Roll a 4 to get some customer service around here.

Boot store is only open on weekends, but you work weekends. Roll a 5 to get a day off.

Boot store requires college degree to purchase. Enroll in night classes. Move back 2 spaces.

"Sorry, can't sell you that pair."

No one working at the boot store speaks your language.

NO

CONGRATS! YOU GOT YOUR— Nope. Get accused of stealing boots. (Miss next turn while calmly looking for receipt.)

Wish you could buy a pair for your mom. She's never had a new pair of boots in her life.

Shit. These boots don't even have straps.

You did it! You've achieved the American Dream!

Damn. Boots are expensive. Apply for the Boot Store credit card. Roll a 6 to get approved.

Valid ID required to buy boots. Give them your Tribal ID, but they don't accept it. Move back 2 spaces.

FINISH

Ready to talk about intersectionality?

WKB: It's one of those words that's been swept into the mainstream, and used in all kinds of sloppy ways. It's a buzzword for white people to prove they're not racist, and a boogeyman—

KS: Can we say "boogeyman"? What's the history of that word?

WKB: [*Googles "boogeyman"*] Naw, we're good. But let's put it in the book that you asked me. Anyway, *intersectionality* has become a darling of conservatives who are convinced that it's a dangerous conspiracy of victimization and a plot to replace existing racial hierarchies with new ones.

KS: And also an alien pizza shop global cabal?

WKB: Let's make it absolutely clear who came up with the term and articulated the theory in the first damn place:
Professor Kimberlé Crenshaw, a lawyer (who was part of Anita Hill's defense team in 1991), a college professor at Columbia University and UCLA, and most importantly and critically . . . a Black woman.

In 1989, she wrote a paper called "Demarginalizing the Intersection of Race and Sex: A Black Feminist Critique of Antidiscrimination Doctrine, Feminist Theory and Antiracist Politics." (Bonus points if you remember the name of that paper next time you're at a party.)

KS: The paper is theoretical, daring, and brilliant. It's also available for you to read on the internet. TL;DR: intersectionality is the idea that all people have multiple intersecting identities, and thus experience discrimination differently. Crenshaw argues that in legal cases about discrimination it is irresponsible for the courts to separate a Black woman's Blackness from her woman-ness. Doing so ignores the specific challenges that Black women face as a group. She offers *intersectionality* as a legal framework that acts "as a prism to bring to light dynamics within discrimination law that weren't being appreciated by the courts." Crenshaw's paper and ideas were central to the development of critical race theory, a form of legal scholarship taught in law schools and other graduate-level programs.

WKB: Intersectionality helps us understand that multiple identities don't exist as separate identities—and that shouldn't be ignored in the court of law, especially in cases concerning discrimination. In other words: There's no such thing as "Which part of you is being discriminated against today?"

One of the most important things to understand about systems of privilege is how they work together. How they *intersect*. White privilege is not the same as class privilege, but you can definitely have both—or just one. Having one kind of privilege doesn't negate other kinds, or cancel out the power you have.

KS: This is one of the key ways that white women, and white feminists in particular, continue to fail: We ignore race, and believe in some universal category of "woman" and "sisterhood" as if we're all experiencing gender in the same ways. And just because you have one identity in common, doesn't mean your experiences are entirely analogous.

DO THE READING

For more reading on intersectionality and critical race theory, check out:

- *Critical Race Theory: The Key Writings That Formed the Movement*, edited by Kimberlé Crenshaw, Neil Gotanda, Gary Peller, and Kendall Thomas

- *The Derrick Bell Reader* by Richard Delgado

- *Faces at the Bottom of the Well* by Derrick Bell

- The article "Toward a Critical Race Theory of Education" by Gloria Ladson-Billings and William F. Tate IV

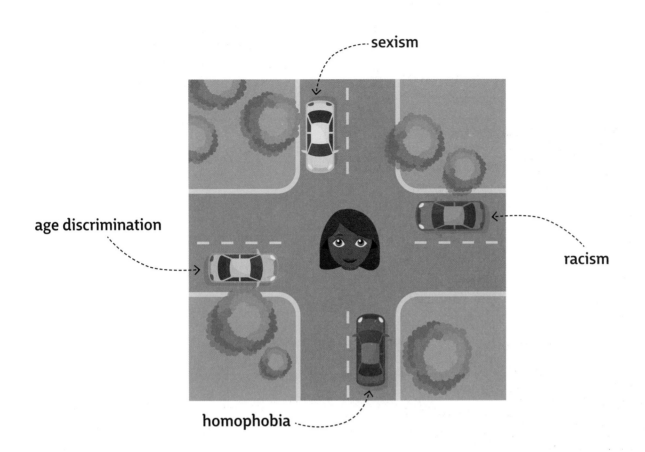

sexism

age discrimination

racism

homophobia

"Consider an analogy to traffic in an intersection, coming and going in all four directions. Discrimination, like traffic through an intersection, may flow in one direction, and it may flow in another.

"If an accident happens in an intersection, it can be caused by cars traveling from any number of directions and, sometimes, from all of them. Similarly, if a Black woman is harmed because she is in the intersection, her injury could result from sex discrimination or race discrimination.

"But it is not always easy to reconstruct an accident: Sometimes the skid marks and the injuries simply indicate that they occurred simultaneously, frustrating efforts to determine which driver caused the harm. In these cases the tendency seems to be that no driver is held responsible, no treatment is administered, and the involved parties simply get back in their cars and zoom away."

—KIMBERLÉ CRENSHAW
from "Demarginalizing the
Intersection of Race and Sex"

We asked people to share real-world examples of how they leverage their privileges to interrupt, challenge, and ultimately end white supremacy.

"I've bought my **BIPOC friends dinner** when they've experienced shitty microaggressions at work."

"I post an annual list of nonprofits run by **Black women** that my friends should donate money to."

"When I see police pulling over somebody who is not white I make an effort to pull over or stop and watc[h] Since my local police don't wear body cameras, I will be the camera for them until they are more accountable."

"As the descendant of enslavers, **I've gone through my family's extensive documentation to find the names, ages, and families of the people my family enslaved** and either pass it on to the descendants or make it publicly available to descendants who are looking for their ancestors."

"When I'm asked to speak on panels, **I check to see how diverse the panel really is**. If it's not, I offer to step back and introduce the organizers to a wealth of colleagues who would better fill my spot."

"After a string of attacks against elderly Asian people in my community, **I approached my neighbor and asked if I could walk with her to the local market.**"

"I leverage my white privilege at work by insisting that every candidate pool has AT LEAST two people of color and/or women candidates. I've asked HR to make this a requirement, and to implement antibias training in the interview and promotion processes."

"I met with a white male **founder of a really influential philanthropic organization to tell him the honest truth** of the ways in which I think his well-intentioned organization is causing harm."

"When I'm able, **I leverage my economic privilege** by leaving really big tips to BIPOC service workers."

"**I speak/greet people in their language** if I'm able to."

"My company has a Black Employee Resource Committee, and a lot of well-meaning white folks joined to support Black colleagues. This was great, but in order to maintain the integrity of that group as a safe space for Black employees **we started pulling white folks out of that space, and into an Ally Accountability Group, which has actionable plans.**"

"I use my educational privilege to remove barriers for people with disabilities."

"I'm a teacher of teenagers and I **give them space to say what they need to say in their art, in their speech**, and in their writing. Sometimes people just need to be heard."

"I have a large social media following so **I use it a lot to amplify the efforts and pages of BIPOC content creators and organizers.**"

"If I'm learning from the social media account of a BIPOC and their bio includes a way to pay them, I do."

"As a white-presenting Black person, this is my *life*. I constantly leverage my privilege to call white people out for racist things they say and do in my presence, because they assume I'm white."

What have you done to **leverage your privilege**?

"I use my privilege as a business owner to provide jobs and mentorship to BIPOC youth so that they can see someone who looks like them in a leadership position."

"I'm not rich, but I'm financially stable, and **I've helped a few of my BIPOC former high school students with their expenses,** including community college tuition, rent, and bills. They're navigating adulthood without family support. I do it quietly, without asking questions or offering advice, and I expect nothing in return."

"I mentor Black junior staff who aren't getting the opportunities to get promoted, and help create those opportunities by doing things like co-authoring publications with them as the first author."

"I went to my Black neighbor's house when there were two white policemen out front. **I didn't leave until I made eye contact with her and asked if everything was OK**. She said it was, so I left, but still stayed nearby."

So.
You've acknowledged your privileges. You've processed some feelings around that (hopefully). You've thought about your access, your influence, your power. You've read a bunch of examples of how others leverage their privilege in service of equity, justice, and community. Now let's put it on paper.

1 Start small!

My privilege:

_____

Gives me access to:

_____

And I commit to:

_____

The first step is:

_____

I'll start:

_____

2 I can do this now!

My privilege: _____

_____

Gives me access to: _____

_____

And I commit to:

_____

_____

The first step is:

_____

_____

I'll start:

_____

_____

3 Makes me nervous but I'll try . . .

My privilege: _____

Gives me access to: _____

And I commit to: _____

The first step is: _____

I'll start: _____

When you get to the end of the book, come back and check this page!
Have you done any of it?
Did you get new ideas?

SHUT UP AND DRIBBLE, MY ASS By Adesina O. Koiki

The people who inspired this puzzle work hard on the court and field—and off as well. They're part of the long tradition of athletes who leverage their privilege by using their platforms to advocate for change and racial justice. They've faced criticism and ridicule, and some have sacrificed their careers. But they all know that silence in the face of injustice is not acceptable.

ACROSS

1 Experiencing writer's block, say
6 *The Equalizer* network
9 Many a baby's first word
13 Sam on *The Muppet Show*, e.g.
14 Genuine
16 Egyptian goddess of fertility
17 In explaining his 2016 stance, he said, "To me, this is bigger than football and it would be selfish on my part to look the other way."
20 Smartphone card
21 CrossFitter's six-pack
22 Elements of a cacophony
23 "Friend," in Montréal
25 *Illmatic* rapper
26 With 45-Across, a way for prominent Black influencers to address civil unrest
32 Outlaw
33 Enclose securely
34 Site for handmade gifts
37 They may grow into tulips
39 Bagel topping
40 Cropped up
41 Italian greeting or farewell
42 The "W" in WNBA
44 ___and outs
45 See 26-Across
48 Fabrication
49 Muscular twitch
50 First segment of a play
53 "Didn't I freakin' tell you?"
55 Takeoff guess, for short
58 1967 assembly of prominent Black athletes concerning Muhammad Ali's refusal to be drafted into the US Army
62 Copenhagen native
63 Unexpected drawback
64 Yellowish-red tropical fruit
65 Capt.'s inferior in the Navy
66 Gibbon, for example
67 Restless

DOWN

1 Its members include the Tigers of Auburn, LSU, and Missouri (abbr.)
2 New Mexico art community
3 Citrus fruit that tastes much better than it sounds

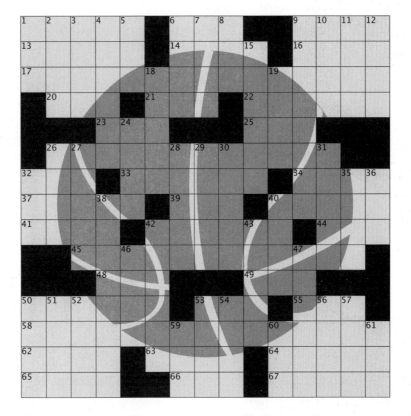

4 Most intense moment
5 ___Norton, former heavyweight champion in boxing (father) or Super Bowl champion (son)
6 Crustacean with pincers
7 Birds' partner in a coming-of-age metaphor
8 Maple tree fluid
9 Dr. Martin Luther King Jr., by occupation
10 Yard sale disclaimer
11 Lab test subjects, often
12 Poses a question
15 Surname of one of the Beatles
18 Clinton's 2016 running mate
19 Raucous crowd's sound
24 Fail to notice
26 Second-largest Hawaiian island
27 Relative by marriage
28 Lively ballroom dance named after a horse's gait
29 Video playback speed, for short
30 Digital image component
31 Unlikely to explode?
32 *Doctor Who* channel

35 IDs on tax forms
36 Affirmative answer
38 Release one's frustration
40 ___Spumante (sparkling Italian wine)
42 Automobile, informally
43 Casual evenings?
46 Fork's prong
47 Nickname of NBA Hall of Famer George Gervin, with "The"
50 "Highway to Hell" band
51 Happy as a____
52 Look after
53 Member of a cereal box trio
54 Defeat by a small margin
56 Crime-fighting quartet mentored by Master Splinter (abbr.)
57 Snide remarks
59 Santa ___ winds
60 Thurman of *Pulp Fiction*
61 Happy Meal add-in

Answers on page 156

CHAPTER 3

How Did We Get Here?

WE CAN'T DISMANTLE what we don't see. Doing the work requires learning how the racist foundations of the United States are connected to the things we're trying to fix today. In this chapter we'll be visiting different moments in US history in order to:

⇨ Practice seeing how racism is baked into systems and how those systems shape the lives of individuals and communities.

⇨ Design new monuments to celebrate people who did the work.

⇨ Learn to center Black women's voices as part of our ongoing (re)education.

SUPPLIES

PARTNER   PEN/PENCIL   INTERNET   ART SUPPLIES

THIS IS A
PARTNER ACTIVITY

FIND A FRIEND and have them ask you the following questions.
You have 20 minutes to answer them all. You must answer 12 of the
20 questions correctly to pass.

1. What is the supreme law of the land? _____

2. Name one American Indian tribe in the United States. _____

3. Name one of the two longest rivers in the United States. _____

4. Under our Constitution, some powers belong to the federal government. What is one power of the federal government?
_____

5. Why did the United States enter the Korean War? _____

6. There were 13 original colonies. Name 5. _____
_____

7. Dwight D. Eisenhower is famous for many things. Name one. _____

8. How many amendments does the US Constitution have? _____

9. How many voting members are in the House of Representatives? _____

10. We elect a US Senator for how many years? _____

11. The Federalist Papers supported the passage of the US Constitution. Name one of the writers.
_____

12. There are four amendments to the Constitution about who can vote. Describe one of them.
_____

13. Who was president during the Great Depression and World War II? _____

14. What is the name of the national anthem? _____

15. Name one state that borders Canada: _____

16. Name a right that is only for US citizens: _____

17. When was the Constitution written? _____

18. Who is the Chief Justice of the Supreme Court right now? _____

19. How many justices are on the Supreme Court? _____

20. Name one example of an American innovation: _____

Answers on pages 153–4

You just answered 20 of the 128 possible questions from the 2020 version of the US Citizenship and Immigration Services (USCIS) civics test for individuals seeking to become naturalized citizens. The test consists of 20 questions, delivered orally in an interview setting, and is intended to test the person's knowledge of US history and government. Applicants must answer 60 percent of the questions correctly to become an American citizen, and they can access study guides in advance.

Some of the questions have fixed answers (the number of Senators and Supreme Court justices hasn't changed in many years) while others have many possible answers (name any Indigenous American tribe) and are highly subjective. (What is Dwight D. Eisenhower famous for? What is the range of acceptable answers and who determines that?) Possessing an understanding of American history is a requirement for anyone who wants to become a citizen—but what about those of us born into this country? What do we know, what do we learn—and why does it matter?

Naturalization is the legal process by which a noncitizen can become a US citizen. Without the right to naturalize, immigrants cannot receive federal service, cannot vote, and have no political voice or power. The process for becoming a citizen, and the laws surrounding it, have changed many times over the centuries, most often in response to war, the need for labor, and xenophobic bullshit. And from the beginning, those laws determining who gets to be a full citizen of these United States (and who gets to come to the United States) have been intertwined with—you guessed it!—race.

Here's a brief timeline of just some of the key moments in American immigration and citizenship policy through 1965, when immigration quotas stopped favoring those from northern and western Europe. Plenty more has happened since then, but these laws help us understand how we got here.

RACE AND LEGAL citizenship have been connected in the United States since, well, the very first federal law that determined who got to be a citizen: **The Naturalization Act of 1790,** which officially restricted citizenship to "any alien, being a free white person" who had been in the United States for two years. Sorry, everyone else.

1868 **The 14th Amendment guarantees** citizenship to "all persons born or naturalized in the United States"—including Black Americans and enslaved people who had been emancipated after the Civil War.

1870 **The Naturalization Act of 1870** extends citizenship to "aliens of African descent." All others considered "non-white" (including immigrants from Asian countries) are barred from citizenship.

1875 **The California Gold Rush** leads to Chinese immigration, which leads to the first restrictive (racist) immigration law: the Page Act, which blocks laborers from "China, Japan, or any Oriental country," and Asian women thought to be sex workers.

> **DO THE WORK**
>
> - Circle any dates on the timeline that relate to your familiy's history of immigration and/or citizenship.
>
> - Find an organization that works for immigrant rights and become a recurring donor.
>
> - What skills do you have that can be of service to immigrants and refugees? How might you put them to use?

1882 **The Chinese Exclusion Act bans** the entry of workers from China. The 1892 Geary Act requires all Chinese residents to carry a Certificate of Residence to prove their legal status (the earliest iteration of the green card).

1902 **The Chinese Exclusion Act** becomes permanent.

1917 **The Immigration Act of 1917** creates a "Barred Zone" prohibiting all immigration from countries spanning the Middle East to Southeast Asia and expanding the reasons people can be excluded from entry into the United States. It also adds a literacy test intended to reduce European immigration.

1924 To stem the tide of Polish, Irish, Italian, Greek, Slavic, and Jewish immigrants, President Coolidge signs the **Immigration Act of 1924**, establishing quotas that limit immigration from any country to 2 percent of the number of immigrants from that country that were permitted in 1890.

1924 Congress enacts the **Indian Citizenship Act**, granting citizenship to all Native Americans, who were previously excluded from laws regarding birthright citizenship (even though they were, uh, born here). The new law meant that Indigenous people were eligible for military service and federal taxes—but fun fact, the right to vote was governed by state law, with states like Utah and New Mexico withholding voting rights for Indigenous citizens until the late 1950s.

1943 The **Magnuson Act** finally repeals the Chinese Exclusion Act; it allows 105 Chinese immigrants each year.

1952 The **Immigration and Nationality Act of 1952** abolishes direct racial barriers, finally allowing Asians to become naturalized citizens. It allows immigration from independent former colonies in Asia and Africa. It still allocates 85 percent of immigration quotas to Western and Northern Europeans, and Asians remain the only population tracked by race.

1965 The **Immigration and Naturalization Act of 1965** eliminates the national origins formula, opening the door to immigration from Asia and Africa. It lays the ground for the current system of immigration in use today.

Cut out the following pieces. In less than
30 seconds, arrange them to make a human face.

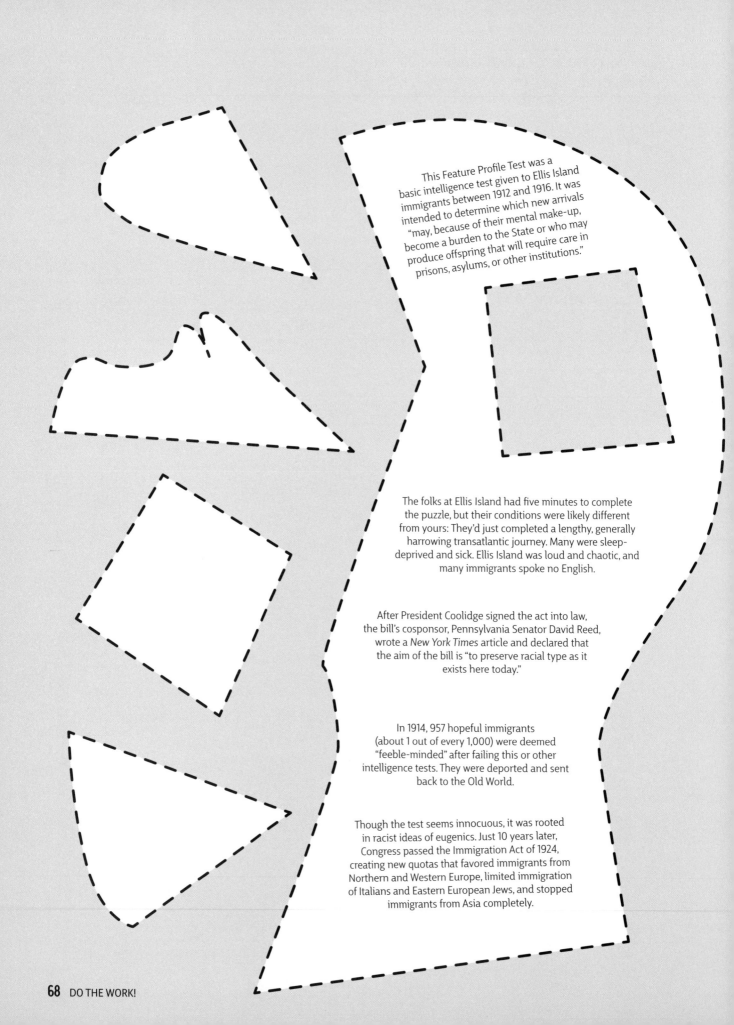

This Feature Profile Test was a basic intelligence test given to Ellis Island immigrants between 1912 and 1916. It was intended to determine which new arrivals "may, because of their mental make-up, become a burden to the State or who may produce offspring that will require care in prisons, asylums, or other institutions."

The folks at Ellis Island had five minutes to complete the puzzle, but their conditions were likely different from yours: They'd just completed a lengthy, generally harrowing transatlantic journey. Many were sleep-deprived and sick. Ellis Island was loud and chaotic, and many immigrants spoke no English.

After President Coolidge signed the act into law, the bill's cosponsor, Pennsylvania Senator David Reed, wrote a *New York Times* article and declared that the aim of the bill is "to preserve racial type as it exists here today."

In 1914, 957 hopeful immigrants (about 1 out of every 1,000) were deemed "feeble-minded" after failing this or other intelligence tests. They were deported and sent back to the Old World.

Though the test seems innocuous, it was rooted in racist ideas of eugenics. Just 10 years later, Congress passed the Immigration Act of 1924, creating new quotas that favored immigrants from Northern and Western Europe, limited immigration of Italians and Eastern European Jews, and stopped immigrants from Asia completely.

So can I be honest for a second?

This book would suck if we weren't being honest, so yes.

WKB: When I was a kid, I hated history. These days I'm the asshole who says things like "I only read historical nonfiction." But back then, I was *not* feeling it. Now I realize that my hatred of history was my hatred of history class. To quote Rage Against the Machine's Zack de la Rocha: "The present curriculum, I put my fist in 'em. Eurocentric, every last one of 'em."

KS: Pretty sure I scrawled that exact same lyric on my binder during my high school history class. And yes! Whenever I hear people say "I hate history!" I'm like "NO! STOP! You hate history *class*! You can't hate *history*. That's like saying you hate *food*, when you just don't like what's being *served*.

WKB: I learned more about American history from reading *The Autobiography of Malcolm X* when I was 18 and Alex Haley's *Roots* when I was in my early twenties than I ever did from any class I took.

KS: And I learned more from the first chapter of Howard Zinn's *A People's History of the United States*.

WKB: Is this the part where we tell them that learning and relearning history is actually a huge part of doing the work?

KS: *[Clears throat, cups hands around mouth]* ANNOUNCEMENT: YOU CAN'T UNDERSTAND THE PRESENT IF YOU DON'T UNDERSTAND THE PAST!

WKB: Are you trying to quote Bob Marley? Bet you wrote that lyric on your notebook as well!

KS: Probably! And not only do we need to understand the past, but we need to understand all the pasts—plural. Not just the ones where America rules and heroic white people saved the day.

WKB: History is like America's highly selective résumé—we really beef up the awards and community service, and tend to leave out the parts where we committed mass genocide.

KS: Well it is hard to get a job when you're a straight-up racist asshole.

WKB + KS: LOLOLOL

KS: Back to history class. Why did we dislike it so much? Why didn't I learn about radical women in history class? Why didn't we learn about enslaved people revolting or resistance groups resisting or white racial justice radical organizing? Why did you get more from Malcolm X and *Roots*?

WKB: Because America picks and chooses the narratives that make it look good, which are usually the stories of white men working hard and accomplishing their goals. American exceptionalism!

KS: Much of which happened because those people relied on racist beliefs to make themselves look exceptional.

WKB: Or while they were actually being exceptional in one area they were being racist asshats in another.

KS: You can't understand America if you don't understand its racist history and how that history connects to everything going on today.

KB: It's all mixed together, baked in America's cake.

KS: You mean our apple pie?

KB: That, too.

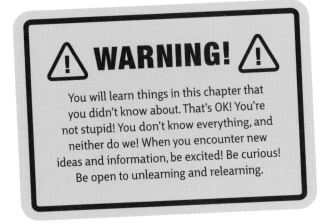

⚠ WARNING! ⚠

You will learn things in this chapter that you didn't know about. That's OK! You're not stupid! You don't know everything, and neither do we! When you encounter new ideas and information, be excited! Be curious! Be open to unlearning and relearning.

READ ALL ABOUT IT!

For a lot of Americans, the study of history stops after high school. But there's so much more to learn!

　We asked two professors of US history to tell us their list of go-to books that everyone should read.

　Here are just some of the titles that Dr. Thanayi Jackson (California Polytechnic State University) and Dr. Gabriel Mendes (Bard College) would like to see on bookshelves. (Cats are optional.) Turn to page 152 for the full list of titles and authors.

What books have YOU read that got you excited about history? They don't have to be nonfiction—we can learn so much from poetry, fiction, plays, and children's books.

DIRECTIONS: Add your titles to the blank spines on the bookshelf, and draw their covers below!

12 Million
**Black
Voices**

Richard Wright

**STUDS
TERKEL**
*HARD
TIMES*

**Southern Horrors
and Other Writings**

THE **MORNING
BREAKS**

THE TRIAL OF
ANGELA DAVIS

BETTINA APTHEKER

MAKING
**GAY
HISTORY**

ERIC MARCUS

**Local
People**

The
Struggle
for
Civil Rights
in
Mississippi

John Dittmer

LIES MY TEACHER TOLD ME | JAMES W. LOEWEN

A DISABILITY
HISTORY *of the*
UNITED STATES

KIM E. NIELSEN

SUZANNE DUNBAR-ORTIZ

A
PEOPLE'S
HISTORY
OF THE
UNITED
STATES

HOWARD
ZINN

**IRON
CAGES**

RACE AND
CULTURE IN
19 TH-CENTURY
AMERICA

REVISED EDITION

RONALD TAKAKI

*American Slavery,
American Freedom*

EDMUND S. MORGAN

BLACK
is a country

W.E.B. DU BOIS

**B L A C K
RECONSTRUCTION
IN AMERICA** 1860-1880

INTRODUCTION BY DAVID LEVERING LEWIS

ZORA NEALE HURSTON
BARRACOON

THE WARMTH
of Other Suns

ISABEL
WILKERSON

*The Apocalypse
of Settler
Colonialism*

The Roots of Slavery,
White Supremacy, and
Capitalism in Seventeenth-
Century North America
and the Caribbean

GERALD HORNE

RACECRAFT
The Soul of Inequality
in American Life

KAREN E. FIELDS AND BARBARA J. FIELDS

**BLACK SKIN,
WHITE MASKS**

FRANTZ FANON

AUTHOR OF *THE WRETCHED OF THE EARTH*

AN
**AFRICAN
AMERICAN**
AND **LATINX
HISTORY**
OF THE UNITED STATES
PAUL ORTIZ

HAYWARD LANES, SCIENTIFIC, HISTORIC EXPERIMENTS | SADIYA HARTMAN

TIYA MILES
TIES THAT BIND

THE STORY OF AN AFRO-CHEROKEE FAMILY
IN SLAVERY AND FREEDOM

Beyond
RESPECTABILITY

THE INTELLECTUAL
THOUGHT OF
RACE WOMEN

BRITTNEY C. COOPER

ANGELA Y. DAVIS | WOMEN RACE & CLASS

ERIC FONER
RECONSTRUCTION
UPDATED EDITION

AMERICA'S UNFINISHED
REVOLUTION
1863-1877

**MARGINS &
MAINSTREAMS**

ASIANS IN AMERICAN HISTORY AND CULTURE

GARY Y. OKIHIRO

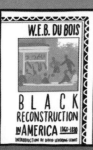

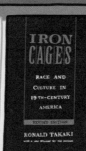

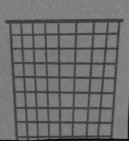
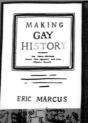

GREAT* MOMENTS IN PRESIDENTIAL HISTORY

Most American children grow up learning heroic facts about the men who've been in charge. Turns out America's presidents have been kinda problematic. Here's a sampling of just some of the things we don't usually learn about our dear leaders.

DIRECTIONS: Match the man to the facts by writing the number next to the text.

A ____ When this president ruined his teeth by cracking walnut shells, his dentures were made from the teeth of those he'd enslaved (along with cow and horse teeth).

B ____ Known for being an antislavery hero and all, but in 1858 definitely said, "There must be the position of superior and inferior, and I as much as any other man am in favor of having the superior position assigned to the white race."

C ____ Ordered the US invasion of Grenada in 1983, authorized the CIA's trafficking of cocaine into the country, pretty much ignored AIDS, and relied heavily on race-baiting and dog-whistle racism, invoking "states' rights" and creating the "welfare queen" stereotype. Also a very mediocre actor.

D ____ Was so opposed to the idea of government actually helping its citizens that he denied aid to the mostly Black riverside communities who'd been devastated in the Great Mississippi Flood of 1927, and refused to even visit the stricken areas.

E ____ Responsible for the deaths of at least 4,000 Cherokee people who were forced from their homes after he signed the Indian Removal Act of 1830.

F ____ Signed the Fugitive Slave Act of 1850, making it legal to literally kidnap free Black people in the North and drag them back into slavery.

G ____ In 1823, he basically invented American imperialism with his own doctrine.

H ____ Considered by many to be the most-criticized president ever (well, until 2016). Drunk at his own inauguration after he accidentally became president, he wrote: "This is a country for white men, and by God, as long as I am President, it shall be a government for white men."

I ____ In 1898, after US forces overthrew the Kingdom of Hawai'i, he annexed it for the profit of white American farmers and businessmen. And tourists!

J ____ "Brownie, you're doing a heck of a job." (History shows that Brownie indeed did not do a "heck of a job." Neither did this president.)

K ____ Passed critical civil rights legislation in the 1960s, but this good ol' boy from Texas was known for his frequent use of the N-word.

L ____ Signed the 1994 crime bill, accelerating mass incarceration by incentivizing states to build more prisons and hand out harsher sentences.

M ____ At a White House dinner in 1954, this president shocked Supreme Court Justice Earl Warren when he said, "These [Southerners] are not bad people. All they are concerned about is to see that their sweet little girls are not required to sit in school alongside some big overgrown Negroes."

N ____ Created an iterative algebraic equation to determine how long it would take to breed the Black out of someone, and said that "Blacks . . . are inferior to the whites in the endowments both of body and mind."

O ____ Literally way too many shitty things to list about this one.

P ____ Took over Haiti! Resegregated the federal government! And the Navy! Publicly questioned the loyalty of "hyphenated Americans"! Stripped Black people from appointed positions of power and replaced them with white Southerners! Submitted a legislative agenda so racist his own Congress said "nope"! Held a screening for *Birth of a Nation* at the White House, which led to the resurgence of the KKK!

Q ____ A lifelong supporter of slavery, he ruthlessly manifested America's racist destiny and in 1846, provoked war with Mexico.

R ____ Labeled the "Deporter-in-Chief" for deporting nearly 3 million people during his eight years in office.

S ____ Before he became president in 1825, he wrote in his diary, "Slavery in a moral sense is an evil; but as connected with commerce it has important uses."

T ____ Signed the 1942 executive order that forcibly imprisoned over 120,000 innocent people of Japanese descent in internment camps.

DRAW THREE FUTURE PRESIDENTS, AND INCLUDE FACTS ABOUT THEM.

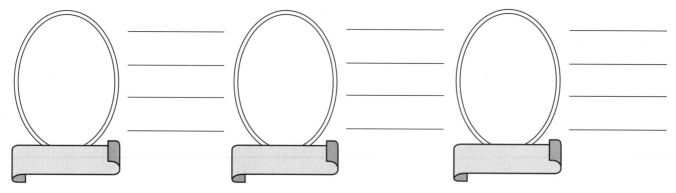

*"Great" as in "Wow! That's a great big amount of racism!"

ANSWERS ON PAGE 154

1 WASHINGTON   3 JEFFERSON   5 MONROE   6 ADAMS   7 JACKSON

11 POLK   13 FILLMORE   16 LINCOLN   17 A. JOHNSON   25 MCKINLEY

28 WILSON   30 COOLIDGE   32 ROOSEVELT   34 EISENHOWER   36 L. B. JOHNSON

40 REAGAN   42 CLINTON   43 BUSH   44 OBAMA   45 TRUMP

PICTURING HISTORY

The images of America that we encounter in history books have a huge impact on our perceptions of what happened, how it happened, and who was there. What photos get included in history books, and which ones get left out? And what do we NOT learn because of these omissions?

Each of these photos depicts a significant moment or figure in American history that we don't often learn about.

DIRECTIONS: Look closely at each one, and do your best to answer the questions.

1. Sumner, MS, 1955. Who are these people and what are they celebrating?

_____

_____

_____

_____

2. Carlisle, PA, 1892. Who are these children?

_____

_____

3. Oakland, CA, 1942. What is happening in this photo? Why is that sign being displayed?

_____

_____

_____

4. Philadelphia, PA, 1985. What happened to this neighborhood?

_____

_____

_____

5. New York City, NY, 1973. Who are they and what are they doing?

_____

_____

_____

6. Washington, DC, likely 1870. Who is this man?

_____

ANSWERS

1. This photo depicts (from L to R) J. W. Milam, Juanita Milam, and Carolyn and Roy Bryant. They're celebrating in front of a crowd of reporters because J. W., Roy, and Carolyn had just been acquitted in the murder of Emmett Till, a 14-year-old Black boy whose mutilated body was found in Mississippi's Tallahatchie River in 1955.

One year later, Milam and Roy Bryant confessed to the murder and sold their story to *Look* magazine.

2. These are the children of the Carlisle Indian School, in Carlisle, PA, in 1892. Carlisle was one of many Indian Boarding Schools run by the Bureau of Indian Affairs. From 1879 until 1918, more than 10,000 Native American children from 140 tribes attended Carlisle, which was run by Col. Richard Henry Pratt, a white man whose motto was "Kill the Indian, save the man." Pratt believed that the only hope for Indigenous people was the annihilation of their cultural identities and total assimilation with white, Christian culture. When students arrived at the schools (usually after being removed from their homes by economic coercion and/or physical force), they were stripped of all signs of tribal life: boys' braids were cut, they were given uniforms and new "white" names (including surnames), and they were forced to speak only English.

3. This photo was taken in Oakland, CA, by the photographer Dorothea Lange, who was working for the War Relocation Authority. The "I AM AN AMERICAN" sign was commissioned and hung by the shop's owner, Tatsuro Matsuda, on December 8, 1941—the day after the attack on Pearl Harbor. On the evening of December 7, Japanese Americans up and down the West Coast started to be rounded up and detained by the FBI as part of a massive campaign of anti-Japanese government paranoia that resulted in Executive Order 9066 and forced the imprisonment of more than 120,000 people of Japanese descent. Lange took this photo in March 1942: Despite the proclamation of citizenship, Matsuda had sold the business and left town. Soon after, he and his wife were sent to an internment camp in Arizona. He never returned to Oakland.

4. This is a photograph of Osage Ave in West Philadelphia. It was taken in 1985, after the Philadelphia police dropped a bomb on its own residents, killing 11 people, destroying 61 homes, and leaving more than 250 homeless. The bombing was an attempt to end a stand-off between the police and a Black separatist liberation group called MOVE, whose members were living in a rowhouse in a mostly Black middle-class neighborhood. When the bomb was dropped it started a fire, and police ordered the fire department to let it burn.

5. This is Marsha P. Johnson (L) and Sylvia Rivera (R) (person in middle unknown) marching in the 1973 Christopher Street Liberation Day parade—the precursor to the Gay Pride parade. The first Christopher Street Liberation Day march took place in 1970, to mark the one-year anniversary of the Stonewall Uprising (the Stonewall Inn is located on Christopher Street).

Marsha and Sylvia were both young trans women of color who were instrumental in the 1969 Stonewall uprising, and the Gay Liberation Movement that followed. They founded STAR (Street Transvestite Action Revolutionaries), an organization that supported unhoused transgender youth, and their radical presence served as a reminder that the people on the front lines of the struggle for LGBTQ+ rights were often young, poor, and Black and brown.

6. This is Hiram Revels, the first Black American to serve in the US Congress. He was appointed in 1870 (back then, state legislatures appointed national senators) and served until 1871. He was one of two Black men appointed to Congress during the Reconstruction era. Though he was born to free Black parents in North Carolina in 1827, Southern Democrats tried to block his appointment by arguing that he'd only become a citizen in 1866, when the Supreme Court overturned the Dred Scott decision.

SEPARATE AND NOT EQUAL By Adesina O. Koiki

This puzzle is inspired by the history of redlining, the discriminatory housing practice that began in the 1930s with maps that divided urban American cities into "good" areas (marked by green blue lines) and "bad" (marked by red lines), segregating communities and initiating decades of financial and social inequity. The words that fit inside the red lines have "bad" connotations, and the words in the green and blue areas are "good."

ACROSS

1 Friendly
5 Flourish added in a barbershop
9 ___ smear
12 Word before rug or code
13 Porch named for a Hawaiian island
14 One of 27 on the Brazilian flag
16 Ratio measuring the potential profit for every dollar invested
18 Prep apples for baking
19 In front
20 Unagi, at a sushi bar
22 Fond du ___, Wisconsin
23 Laugh like Steve Urkel
24 Misplaced optimism
27 Musician/activist Yoko
28 Magazine highlighting African American culture since 1945
30 Basketball Hall of Famer Malone
31 Unit of electrical power
33 Openly queer
34 Expels by force
35 Discriminatory insurance practice denying loans and services to some communities due to their racial makeup
39 On the ___ (honest)
42 Letters following a proof
43 Ginormous
47 It's used by some animals to mark their territory
48 Occupation of Diahann Carroll's character in the groundbreaking TV series *Julia* (1968–1971)
50 Element of a wedding exchange
51 Charlie Brown's catchphrase
53 Bravery
55 Class for some US citizens-to-be: Abbr.
56 Sana'a is its capital: Abbr.
57 Chris Noth's *Sex and the City* role
58 *How the Other Half Lives* author
60 Far from dazzling
64 Jacob's 12
65 Like numerals on a sundial
66 ___ Stadium (New York Mets's home before 2009)
67 Org. implicated in 2013 leaks by Edward Snowden
68 Gym bag emanation

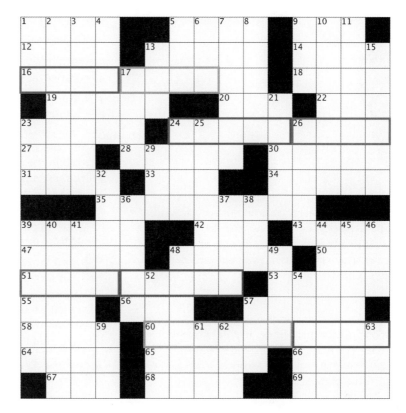

69 Website for handmade gifts

DOWN

1 Combative card game
2 Huffington of HuffPost
3 Take another take
4 One you might not want to meet just yet
5 Something shook in a dog trick
6 Actress de Armas
7 Once in a blue moon
8 High, low, and neap
9 Sony handheld gaming console: Abbr.
10 Bewildered
11 Low wall along the edge of a castle roof
13 Energy-saving bulb, initially
15 Play break
17 By-the-hour charge
21 Clunker of a vehicle
23 Mother to piglets
24 Basketball referee's call
25 Garage sale discovery, perhaps
26 Dancer Julianne or knuckleballer Charlie

29 Dad ___ (physique hardly resembling Mr. Olympia)
32 Become popular on Twitter
36 Lament for the dead
37 Brand with foam-based toys
38 They might be fake on a college campus: Abbr.
39 Some Winter Olympics athletes
40 Shoreline concern
41 Instruments played with bows
44 Electromagnetic radiation responsible for suntans, informally
45 Searches, in modern times
46 NYC area alternative to JFK or LGA
48 Skillful hunter ... or an inept person
49 "Lift ___ voice and sing ..."
52 Quick copy?
54 Exploit, as power
57 Higwh pt.
59 Retiree benefits org.
61 Angsty genre of pop or rap
62 Street paver's substance
63 Celebratory exclamation

Answers on page 156

> **If we want to create systems and institutions that are antiracist, we have to understand *why* they're racist, and *how* that happened.**

KS: When you pay attention to American histories, you understand that nothing happens in an isolated vacuum. When Georgia rewrote its election laws in 2021, after its Black Democratic voters decided the outcome of the 2020 presidential *and* Senate elections, it wasn't unprecedented—it was . . . precedented?

WKB: Is that a word?

KS: When American leaders start blaming global pandemics on China, and anti-Asian hate crimes rise 149 percent in one year, it's not a coincidence. If you know the extensive histories of anti-Asian sentiment in America, you'll get how dangerous this kind of racist scapegoating is.

WKB: You can no longer say "I can't *believe* that!" or "This isn't what America *really* is!" when people talk about America's racist history or current reality.

KS: It's the "I don't see color!" mindset. When you say you *can't believe* that an overt act of racist violence has occured, you're saying—well, you're literally saying you are not able to believe this can happen. And if you pay attention to history, like *at all*, you should absolutely believe it. Let's be real: You should expect it.

WKB: To put it in terms you may understand, be less like Macaulay Culkin at the beginning of *Home Alone* [*makes Macaulay-Culkin-in-Home-Alone face*] and more like Macaulay Culkin when he's got the house wired.

KS: Remember in 2020, when Donald Trump announced he was going to have a rally in Tulsa, Oklahoma, in the midst of the COVID crisis, three weeks after the murder of George Floyd, on *June 19th*?

WKB: My blood pressure's going up just thinking about it.

KS: A lot of folks were furious—and yet, a lot of other folks had no idea why it was a big deal.

WKB: Knowing about Tulsa is a huge part of understanding the racist history of this country. But I get why some might not know about it—*I* never learned about it in school. And I went to a lot of schools!

KS: So, class: What historical insight might inform your understanding of why a Trump rally in Tulsa on June 19th in the midst of the COVID pandemic and a nationwide uprising around racial justice and police brutality was . . . problematic?

WKB: Where to start?

1 Trump, whose events were basically **pep rallies for racism**, chooses . . .

2 **Tulsa, the site of the Tulsa Massacre of 1921, one of the most horrific race-based massacres in American history.** Black folks in Tulsa had been forced into their own section of town, which they turned into a thriving community so successful it became known as "Black Wall Street." And instead of white people being like, "Good for them!" they burned it to the ground and murdered hundreds of men, women, and children.

3 And Trump selects not June 18th, not June 20th, but *June 19th*, aka Juneteenth, aka Jubilee Day, aka Liberation Day, aka the day in 1865 that Black people in Texas finally found out that slavery was over (no Twitter back then—it took two and a half years for news of the Emancipation Proclamation to hit Texas!).

4 And it was a few weeks after the murder of George Floyd. **Protests were sweeping the world**, people were in the *streets*.

5 *And* it was right after the CDC released data showing the **staggering disparities between the rates of COVID deaths** among Black and Latino/a people vs white people.

KS: In other words, if you were paying attention, you were outraged.

WKB: And exhausted.

KS: This goes for so many news stories: When you hear about ICE detainees being sterilized against their will, it's horrifying—but if you know about eugenics, or "Mississippi appendectomies," or *Buck v. Bell*, or the forced sterilization/birth control pill testing on women in Puerto Rico, you'll . . .

WKB: Cry because it's all so messed up?

KS: Yes. Plus you'll see the systemic, institutional racist forces that have led to this moment.

WKB: Can we have another honesty moment?

KS: Lemme guess: You haven't heard of some of the histories I just mentioned?

WKB: I mean, I know about eugenics, and I learned about "Mississippi appendectomies" when I read about Fannie

Lou Hamer for my TV show. But the details on what happened in Puerto Rico? And the court case?

KS: Right. And that's totally OK! I learned about it by doing my own research for my books. Here's the thing: If you haven't heard of any of this, you're not stupid. You're just . . . how do I put this . . . American.

WKB: BOOM!

KS: Which we really can't help. But we can be more than our subpar education—we can be actively curious. We can teach ourselves.

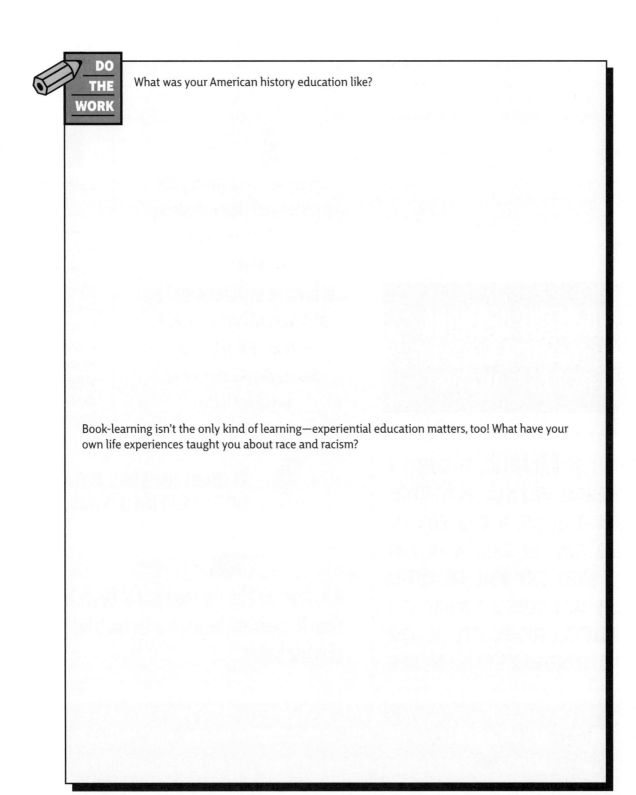

DO THE WORK

What was your American history education like?

Book-learning isn't the only kind of learning—experiential education matters, too! What have your own life experiences taught you about race and racism?

JIM CROW OR JIM FAUX?

Jim Crow laws were state and local laws that legalized racial segregation. They were enacted in many states between 1876 and 1965, from the end of the Civil War to the moment when the Civil Rights Act was finally passed. The laws were a reaction to the post–Civil War Reconstruction period, where newly free Black Southerners began to flourish, building businesses, wealth, community, and political power.

Most of the statutes focused on preventing misegenation, aka interracial marriage, and maintaining strict racial segregation of schools, parks, libraries, hospitals, drinking fountains, buses, trains, restrooms, restaurants, and other public spaces.

In 1896, the Supreme Court established the doctrine of separate but equal in *Plessy v. Ferguson*, after a Black man in New Orleans attempted to sit in a whites-only railway car. This decision legitimized Jim Crow laws, and led to an increase in segregated states across the country—and not just in the South.

From California to North Dakota, Arizona to Texas, racist lawmakers really went for it, making up all kinds of ridiculous laws, leaving no stone untouched by white supremacist fear.

DIRECTIONS: Read the list of Jim Crow laws below. All but one was really on the books—can you spot the "Jim Faux"? Circle it!

 MISSISSIPPI

Any person . . . who shall be guilty of printing, publishing or circulating printed, typewritten or written matter . . . in favor of social equality or of intermarriage between whites and negroes, shall be guilty of a misdemeanor and subject to fine.

 LOUISIANA

The board of trustees shall . . . maintain a separate building . . . on separate ground for the admission, care, instruction, and support of all blind persons of the colored or black race.

NO NATIVE OF CHINA SHALL EVER HAVE THE RIGHT TO VOTE IN THE STATE OF CALIFORNIA

IT SHALL BE **UNLAWFUL** TO CONDUCT A RESTAURANT OR OTHER PLACE FOR THE SERVING OF FOOD IN THE CITY, AT WHICH WHITE AND COLORED PEOPLE ARE SERVED IN THE SAME ROOM, UNLESS SUCH WHITE AND COLORED PERSONS ARE EFFECTUALLY SEPARATED BY A SOLID PARTITION EXTENDING FROM THE FLOOR UPWARD TO A DISTANCE OF SEVEN FEET OR HIGHER.

 GEORGIA NO COLORED BARBER SHALL SERVE AS A BARBER TO WHITE WOMEN OR GIRLS.

 OKLAHOMA

A hearse used for the transport of **Black** bodies must be sanitized before use for the transport of white bodies.

 MARYLAND Any white woman who shall suffer or permit herself to be got with child by a **Negro** or **Mulatto** . . . shall be sentenced to the penitentiary for not less than eighteen months.

GEORGIA It shall be unlawful for any amateur white baseball team to play baseball on any vacant lot or baseball diamond within two blocks of a playground devoted to the Negro race.

 **WYOMING**

All marriages of white persons with Negroes, Mulattos, Mongolians, or Malaya hereafter contracted in the State of Wyoming are and shall be illegal and void.

 **ALABAMA**

IT SHALL BE UNLAWFUL FOR A **NEGRO** AND WHITE PERSON TO PLAY TOGETHER OR IN COMPANY WITH EACH OTHER AT ANY GAME OF POOL OR BILLIARDS.

 SOUTH CAROLINA

It shall be unlawful for any parent, relative, or other white person in this State ... to dispose of, give or surrender such white child permanently into the custody, control, maintenance, or support, of a Negro.

 LOUISIANA

All circuses, shows, and tent exhibitions, to which the attendance of ... more than one race is invited or expected to attend **shall provide for the convenience of its patrons not less than two ticket offices with individual ticket sellers,** and not less than two entrances to the said performance.

 NORTH CAROLINA

SCHOOL TEXTBOOKS SHALL NOT BE INTERCHANGEABLE BETWEEN THE WHITE AND COLORED SCHOOLS, BUT SHALL CONTINUE TO BE USED BY THE RACE FIRST USING THEM.

 ARKANSAS

It shall be unlawful for any white prisoner to be handcuffed or otherwise chained or tied to a negro prisoner.

 FLORIDA

Any Negro man and white woman, or any white man and Negro woman, who are not married to each other, who shall habitually live in and occupy in the nighttime the same room shall each be punished by imprisonment. **Or** by fine.

DO THE READING

The New Jim Crow by Michelle Alexander

ANSWER: The "Jim Faux" is the Oklahoma law about the hearse—in fact, the law stated that there must be entirely separate hearses for the transport of Black and white bodies.

COLOR BY NUMBERS!

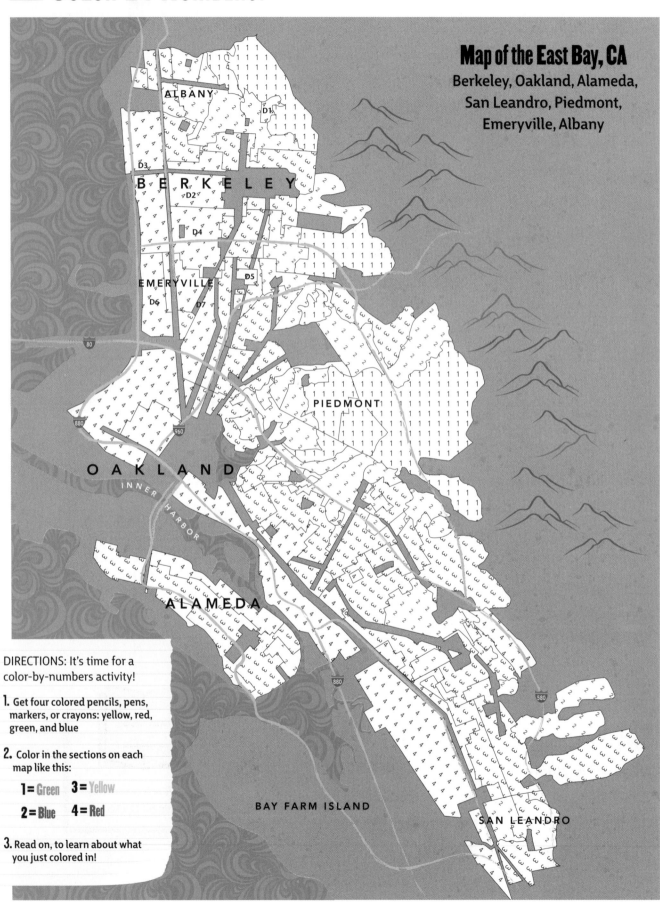

Map of the East Bay, CA
Berkeley, Oakland, Alameda,
San Leandro, Piedmont,
Emeryville, Albany

DIRECTIONS: It's time for a
color-by-numbers activity!

1. Get four colored pencils, pens,
   markers, or crayons: yellow, red,
   green, and blue

2. Color in the sections on each
   map like this:

   1 = Green   3 = Yellow

   2 = Blue   4 = Red

3. Read on, to learn about what
   you just colored in!

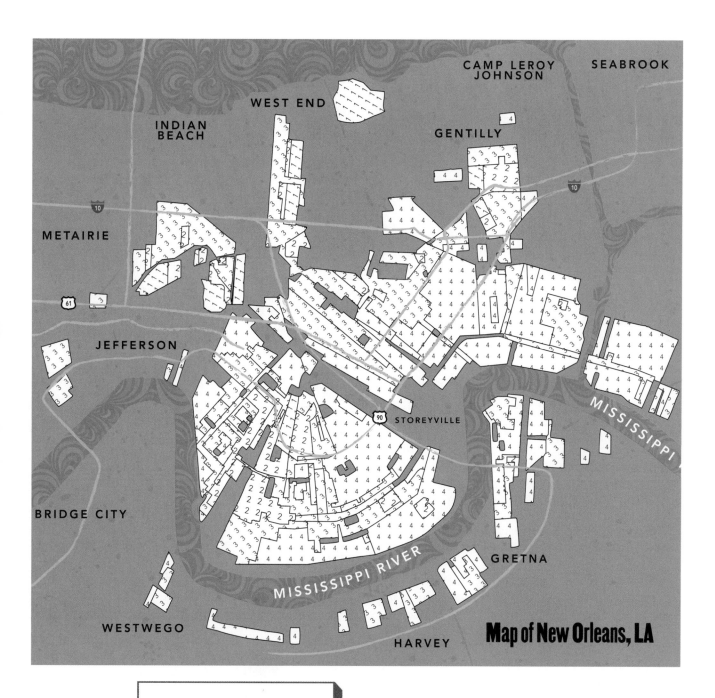

Map of New Orleans, LA

You just colored in some of America's most glaring examples of racism: redlining!

KS: These maps—and their color-coded systems—were just two of the hundreds created in the late 1930s by the Home Owners' Loan Corporation (HOLC), a New Deal program created to stabilize the mortgage system, and block generations of Black families from building equity and generational wealth. (OK, that last part wasn't a stated goal of the HOLC. But that's how systemic racism works!)

WKB: After the Great Depression, HOLC refinanced over a million homes, issuing low-interest, long-term loans to thousands of new homeowners. But not everyone had access to these loans. Because of the maps.

KS: These maps were drawn by teams of real estate professionals who "graded" the perceived lending risks of 239 American cities. Each city was divided into zones based on the racial and class makeup of the people who lived there—and the opinions of the (white) person doing the grading. (The National Association of Real Estate Brokers, 1922 "Code of Ethics" states: "A Realtor should never be instrumental in introducing into a neighborhood . . . members of any race or nationality . . . whose presence will clearly be detrimental to property values.")

WKB: Green zones were the "A" neighborhoods, described as "best" and "desirable." Blue zones were "B": not perfect, but "still desirable." Yellow zones were kinda dicey—they got a "C." And red zones got a "D:" Their Black, immigrant, poor, and other "undesirable" (sometimes including Jewish and Catholic) residents were deemed "hazardous" and "declining." The color red was a clear warning to lenders to avoid issuing loans in these areas. This process came to be known as "redlining."

KS: A 1935 Federal Housing Authority Underwriting Manual declared the importance of protecting against "adverse influences" when creating and enforcing zoning regulations. The most important "adverse influences"? "Infiltration of inharmonious racial or nationality group." (Also: "the presence of smoke, odors, fog, etc.")

WKB: Home ownership is the number one method of accumulating wealth in America. In many ways, the maps became self-fulfilling prophecies: Already challenged neighborhoods that could have improved never got the chance. Instead, they were starved of investment and isolated from potential economic growth. Without access to credit, individuals often fell prey to predatory lenders. Existing homeowners couldn't get access to loans to do home improvements. Commercial investors avoided these neighborhoods. Property values suffered, which affected property taxes, which affected funding for public schools in many cities.

KS: The effects of redlining piled up, impacting cities and communities for decades. After World War II, the maps were used by the Veterans Administration and FHA to determine who should get home loans, thus blocking many people of color from being able to buy homes in the suburban housing developments built in the '40s, '50s, and '60s. Private banks adopted the neighborhood identification system, and continued the practice of denying loans in "risky" areas. The 1968 Fair Housing Act finally prohibited housing discrimination based on race—but an entire generation of BIPOC families had been denied the opportunity to gain the wealth and equity needed to buy into the housing market.

WKB: In the twenty-first century, race remains far more important than income when it comes to who lives where—and what they get access to. Rich and poor white households typically live in neighborhoods that are more than 80 percent white. Black and Latino/a families, regardless of their income levels, typically live in neighborhoods that are disproportionately nonwhite. In addition to racial discrimination in the housing market, researchers cite the disparity in accumulated wealth (cash savings, retirement accounts, home equity) as one of the primary factors of America's high levels of racial segregation in housing.

KS: Today, nearly 75 percent of the historically "red" neighborhoods are still low- to moderate-income areas, with people of color living in nearly 64 percent of those neighborhoods.

WKB: Current residents of Oakland zones marked as "hazardous" in the 1930s are more than twice as likely to visit the ER for asthma-related issues due to high levels of environmental pollution. The devastation of Hurricane Katrina disproportionately impacted Black residents living in vulnerable, low-lying, formerly redlined neighborhoods.

KS: From Detroit to Chicago to Los Angeles, once-redlined communities continue to grapple with the lasting impacts, including increased health risks, underfunded schools, less access to fresh foods, limited job opportunities, and the increasing threats of the climate crisis. Add to that the social stigma of living in "one of those" neighborhoods, and the damage is clear.

DO THE WORK

• Learn more about redlining and histories of racist housing policies in your city! There are numerous mapping projects available online, and all 289 HOLC maps have been digitized.

• Once you find that information, apply it to what you know about your city now.

How has the history of housing policy in your city impacted current housing issues and policy? How has your own neighborhood been impacted?

• Use this historical knowledge to inform any actions you take to pursue housing equity in your town!

LOOK IT UP!
- **Blockbusting**
- **Restrictive covenants**
- **Exclusionary zoning**

PACKING, CRACKING, AND CONNECTING THE DOTS!

DIRECTIONS: Connect the dots on both of the images below.

Area of Detail

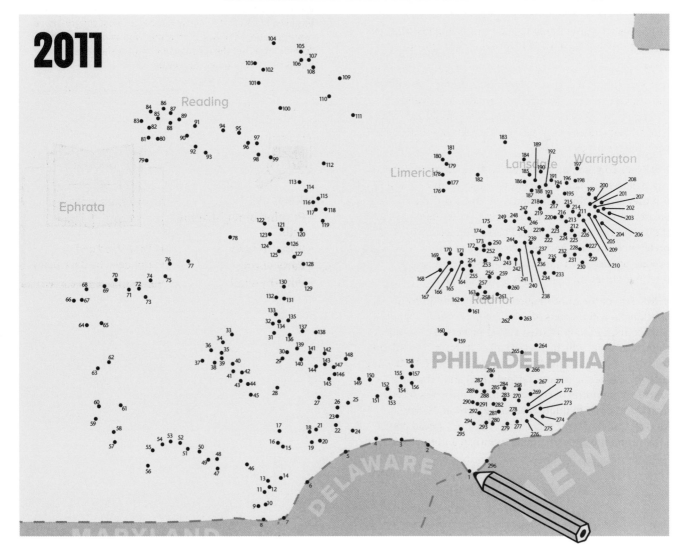

KS: Behold! You just outlined two versions of the same Congressional district: Pennsylvania's 7th, one of America's finest examples of gerrymandering! **Gerrymandering is the manipulation of electoral maps for political advantage.**

WKB: The 7th is notorious for how it's been cracked, contorted, and redrawn over six decades, stretching across five counties and 26 municipalities, from the Philadelphia suburbs out to Amish farm country—all in favor of maintaining political control and minimizing the power of Black and poor voters.

KS: In order to pull in rural (read: more conservative) voters *and* to dilute the power of urban voters, the district bisects a cul-de-sac, crosses an elementary school playground, and at one point, is as wide as a parking lot at a surf 'n' turf restaurant. It even earned a nickname: "Goofy kicking Donald Duck," since if you squint it kinda looks like one Disney character kicking the other in the ass.

WKB: In 2018, the Pennsylvania Supreme Court ruled that the district lines "clearly, plainly, and palpably" violated the state's constitution by unfairly favoring the Republicans who drew them. When lawmakers couldn't agree on new boundaries, the court issued new ones, eliminating 1,100 miles of sprawling borders to create a more compact, contiguous, and balanced district.

KS: So how did any of that happen in the first place?! Let's connect some more dots and understand the history. . . .

WKB: Gerrymandering dates back to 1812, when journalists reacted to redistricting efforts in Massachusetts. One of the districts on the new map, which favored Governor Eldridge Gerry, looked like a strange salamander with wings. Salamander + Gov. Gerry = a neologism that's still very much with us today.

KS: Every 10 years, US states redraw their electoral districts based on census data. These lines on a map can look absurd, but they have serious consequences. In theory, if districts are drawn fairly, the public can elect representatives fairly. If district lines are manipulated based on race, party preference, income, and perceived ways of voting, the process unfairly favors one party over the other and disenfranchises voters—usually voters of color.

WKB: Two of the most frequently used techniques are "packing"—when voters of color are packed into a single district in order to limit their voting power (like San Juan County in Utah, which "packed" all of its Navajo population into one of three voting districts, despite Native folks making up over half of the county's population) and "cracking"— where communities of color are broken up across several districts in order to dilute their voting power. "Goofy kicking Donald Duck" is cracking: The lines spread poor urban communities out among suburban and rural areas.

KS: Is gerrymandering legal? Yes. Kind of. It's complicated. In 1995, the Supreme Court held that racial gerrymandering is a violation of constitutional rights, and they've upheld decisions against redistricting that are *clearly* race-based. But many cases are . . . murky. Redistricting is legal, and the court has struggled to really define which methods of partisan gerrymandering might be unconstitutional. It's . . . a work in progress.

YOUR TURN!

What do you know about your congressional district? What does it look like? How big is it? How many cities does it cover? Do you know what its number is? And who represents you?

REMINDER:

Voter suppression didn't start with gerrymandering—it was enshrined in the Constitution, which only included the rights of white men, and counted Black men as ⅗ of a person. Thanks to Southern enslavers who wanted to count enslaved Blacks in the census in order to boost congressional representation, and Northern whites who said "nope." Their "compromise" set the census value of an enslaved person as 60 percent of the value of a free person.

LOOK IT UP!
- **Purging of registration rolls**
- **Voter ID laws**
- **Early voting**
- **Vote-by-mail**

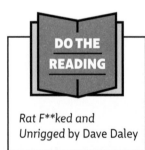

DO THE READING

Rat F**ked and *Unrigged* by Dave Daley

DO THE WORK

DIRECTIONS: Look up your congressional district and draw or paste in images to show how it's evolved.

1950

2000

TODAY

OK, CLASS! IT'S ... MATH TIME!

WKB: Welcome to math class, dear readers!

KS: But we're not teaching this one. We brought in an expert.

WKB: We're turning this part of the book over to Professor Nathan Alexander of Morehouse College.

KS: Wait, stop, don't skip this page because you "don't like math." Try to stick it out and see what you can learn.

PROF. NATE: Greetings class! I'm Prof. Nathan Alexander. For this activity, we're going to look at a timeline of American history and explore how mathematics can work as a lens to help us understand race, class, segregation, and more. See, math is powerful. It can provide a lens into trends that can prompt more focused, local analyses and conversation. In a data-driven culture that routinely doubts and rejects the testimonies and lived experiences of people of color, math can offer proof of the ways that systemic racism works.

WKB: In other words, math shows that they *know* what they're doing.

There's a lot of info on these pages! Feel free to use scratch paper so you can show your work.

Name: _____   Date: ___/___/___

DIRECTIONS: Answer each question along the timeline.

1619

Chattel slavery begins in the United States

WARM-UP: On August 20, 1619, "20 and odd" Angolans were kidnapped by the Portuguese and then sold to English Colonists. It would be 246 years before chattel slavery would be abolished. In what year was chattel slavery legally abolished in the United States?

SUM: 1619
          + 246
_____

1524
Mystery of the first enslaved Africans

PROBLEM #1: An estimated 12.5 million Africans were transported to the Americas during the legal trade of enslaved people, starting as early as 1525. Of those stolen, 10.7 million survived the Middle Passage. Those enslaved were not allowed to read or write, which included learning mathematics. Instead, they cleared and cultivated farmlands in the western hemisphere well into the Jim Crow era and beyond. About 388,000* enslaved and surviving Africans were transported to what is now known as the United States. Based on these estimates, what percent of enslaved Africans were transported to the Untied States?

ESTIMATE: 388,000/10,700,000 =

* Estimate provided by Trans-Atlantic Slave Trade Data

1719

1739
Stono Rebellion

PROBLEM #2: In the United States, a state's population was once determined by the Three-fifths Compromise as a result of the 1787 Constitutional Convention. Despite their status as citizens, the 1790 census shows that Virginia, for example, held an enslaved population of 292,627 out of 746,610 total individuals. What was the population of enslaved Africans used for representation in Virginia?

CALCULATE: 3/5 x 292,627 =

1787
Three-fifths Compromise

PROBLEM #4: Despite progress in the legal sector during the civil rights movement, social status and de facto segregation resulted in the many ongoing political struggles for nonwhite, non-male, economically and socially vulnerable communities. Coming to a better understanding of these struggles has increasingly been supported by statistics, modeling, and mathematics. Modeling in mathematics takes a real-world problem and transforms it using mathematical terms and tools. For example, quantifying the impact of housing crises has allowed new insights into similarities in housing injustices across the nation—such as redlining, gerrymandering, and gentrification.

CALCULATE:
The interstate system was often routed through Black and brown communities. Based on the drawings, what percentage of this neighborhood's original housing was demolished?

⌂ = 50 homes

2119
Welcome to the 22nd century! The future is now!

PROBLEM #5: Critical Thinking: Think hard about the ways that we will depend on numbers, mathematics, and the sciences to transform into a more justice-oriented world as we approach the twenty-second century. What are some examples of how we can use numbers to combat injustice? In doing so, how can you more actively promote a positive view of mathematics—beyond "it's hard."

How can you support advancing mathematics for racial justice?

PROBLEM #3:
Mass incarceration in the United States is a major issue. The belief that slavery ended around Black reconstruction has been debunked by researchers and explored through the many names that slavery has gone by since. Specifically, the creation of new institutions, such as carceral systems, has been used to deny freedom to citizens due to their race. The PRISON INDUSTRIAL COMPLEX is one of the major factors in the Untied States's legal web of injustice. The #abolishprisons movement is an example of the pushback against these systems.

2019

CALCULATE: The United States has the highest rate of incarceration globally. In 2021, this rate was 698 prisoners per 100,000 population. If the current population of the United States were approximately 335,000,000, what is the expected number of US prisoners based on the 2021 incarceration rate?

ΔΕΘ ΚΑΨ ΩΨΦ ΑΚΑ
ΦΒΕ   ΑΦΑ

1919

ΖΦΒ
ΕΓΡ
ΙΦΘ

The Atlanta University Studies (1896–1947) by W. E. B. DuBois

1881
Tuskegee Institute founded by Booker T. Washington

Southern Horrors (1892) and the Red Record (1895) by Ida B. Wells-Barnett

1865
Jim Crow and the segregation of public systems

1819
Key abolition movements

Chattel Slavery "abolished" by the 13th amendment

DO THE WORK

• Please, and I beg you, don't just do the calculations and stop there. Use these math problems to explore the injustices rooted in the numbers.

• Take care with using numbers to "dunk" on anyone or try to argue it as "truth." Without context and critical thought, numbers can be very dangerous because they have material consequences.

• Question the statistics that you read and utilize. All is not what is measured.

• Do more critical mathematics!

Learning and relearning and unlearning histories definitely includes facing the bad stuff, but it's also about the empowering histories.

WKB: There are people and groups and organizations and coalitions they didn't teach you about, because they're not the right kind of heroes. They remind us not just that there was resistance, but that there was something to resist.

KS: We clearly want you to do the work of learning the horrific histories. But we want you to learn all the stuff they never taught you. The rebellion, the resistance, the joy, and triumph.

WKB: With my daughters, I realized that I have to make sure they read books about Black people who've achieved amazing things . . . and also fought racism. And I also have

 HIDDEN PICTURES

Black Americans have been innovating and inventing for centuries—and often not getting credit (or cash).

DIRECTIONS: Let's practice seeing the contributions of Black inventors by finding their creations that are hidden in the cookout.

to make sure that they read books about Black people who fought racism . . . and achieved amazing things.

Basically, I want to make sure my daughters know about **Harriet Tubman** and **Dr. Mae Jemison**. – – – – – – Harriet Tubman's whole life was about confronting and overcoming racism and helping other Black folks do the same. She escaped enslavement—and then went back to help others. It wasn't a sport but it was harder than any other athletic achievement you can think of.

When Dr. Mae Jemison was a child she wanted to grow up and be a dancer and

an astronaut. And she grew up to be . . . a dancer and an astronaut! Turns out she was the first Black woman in space. (Maybe even the first dancer in space, too.) As a little girl she wasn't thinking as much about the "Black" part as she was about the "I want to go into space!" part. But both are important to her story. And I can see that in my daughters' eyes.

Ice-cream scooper
(Alfred L. Cralle)

Ironing board
(Sarah Boone)

Traffic light
(Garrett Morgan)

Longer-lasting Light Bulb
(Lewis Latimer)

Rock 'n' roll
(Sister Rosetta Tharpe)

Hairbrush
(Lyda D. Newman)

Gas mask
(Garrett Morgan)

Potato chips
(George Crum)

Lock
(W. A. Martin)

Blimp
(John F. Pickering)

Golf tee
(Dr. George Grant)

Dustpan
(Lloyd Ray)

Curling iron
(Theora Stephens)

Mailbox
(Philip B. Downing)

Moderna COVID vaccine
(Dr. Kizzmekia Corbett)

Toilet
(Lewis Latimer)

Caller ID
(Dr. Shirley Jackson)

Folding Chair
(Nathaniel Alexander)

Super Soaker
(Lonnie Johnson)

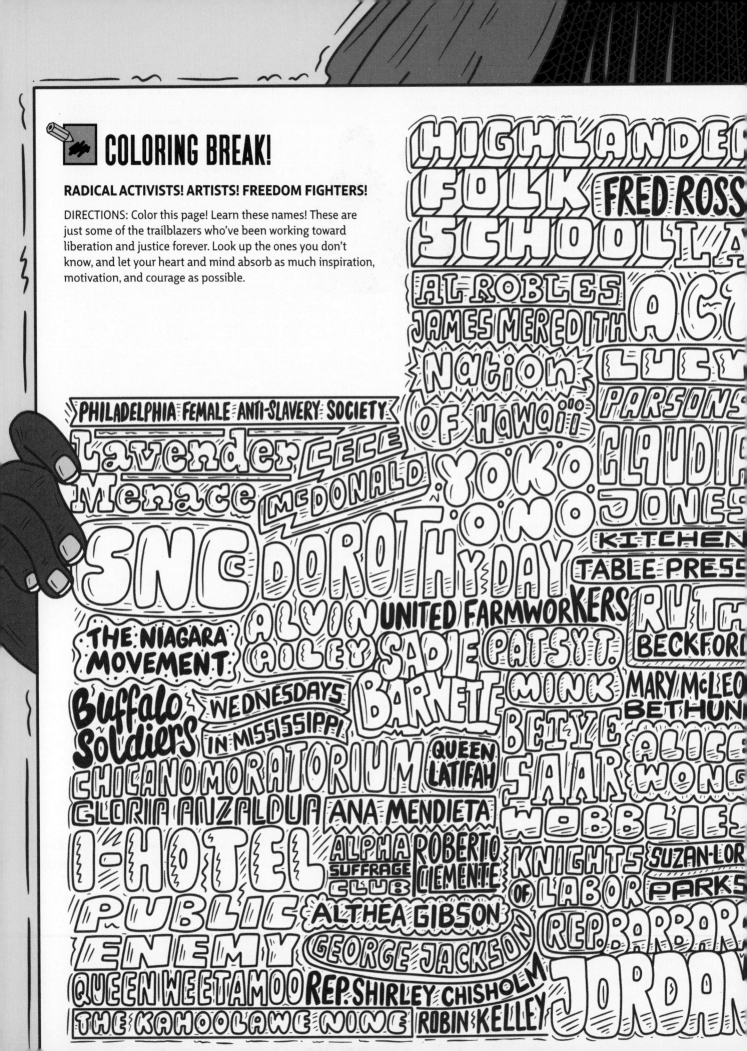

COLORING BREAK!

RADICAL ACTIVISTS! ARTISTS! FREEDOM FIGHTERS!

DIRECTIONS: Color this page! Learn these names! These are just some of the trailblazers who've been working toward liberation and justice forever. Look up the ones you don't know, and let your heart and mind absorb as much inspiration, motivation, and courage as possible.

HIGHLANDER FOLK SCHOOL
FRED ROSS
AL ROBLES
JAMES MEREDITH
Nation of Hawaii
ACT
LUCY PARSONS
CLAUDIA JONES
KITCHEN TABLE PRESS
PHILADELPHIA FEMALE ANTI-SLAVERY SOCIETY
Lavender Menace
CECE McDONALD
YOKO ONO
SNCC
DOROTHY DAY
ALVIN AILEY
UNITED FARMWORKERS
RUTH BECKFORD
THE NIAGARA MOVEMENT
SADIE BARNETT
PATSY T. MINK
MARY McLEOD BETHUNE
Buffalo Soldiers
WEDNESDAYS IN MISSISSIPPI
BETYE SAAR
ALICE WONG
CHICANO MORATORIUM
QUEEN LATIFAH
GLORIA ANZALDUA
ANA MENDIETA
WOBBLIES
I-HOTEL
ALPHA SUFFRAGE CLUB
ROBERTO CLEMENTE
KNIGHTS OF LABOR
SUZAN-LORI PARKS
PUBLIC ENEMY
ALTHEA GIBSON
GEORGE JACKSON
REP. BARBARA JORDAN
QUEEN WEETAMOO
REP. SHIRLEY CHISHOLM
THE KAHOOLAWE NINE
ROBIN KELLEY

HONOR YOUR HEROES

There are lots of amazing, not-shitty figures in American history, and they all have names. We also have a lot of public spaces, schools, parks, sports teams, roads, and buildings. Do we need multiple Woodrow Wilson Middle Schools and parks named after Andrew Jackson in every town? Can we mix it up a bit?

Monuments and statues and street names *matter*. When a statue stands in a public square it confers legitimacy and honor. When a school is named for a historical figure it tells the students: "This person is a *big deal*." These names and figures get cemented in our sense of Important People and Histories.

Radical antiracist freedom fighters aren't usually high on the list for street names and public monuments. But what if they *were*?

DIRECTIONS: Pick some people from the previous page and make them a monument! Or pick one of your own personal heroes!

This **statue of J. Marion Sims**, "the father of modern gynecology" was removed from New York's Central Park in 2018, after an outcry over the fact that Sims did his "research" without consent, on the unanesthetized bodies of enslaved Black women. Who would you replace him with?

RENAME THIS SCHOOL

The debate over keeping/removing monuments to Confederate generals has been ongoing in many cities and states for decades. Most Confederate monuments were erected between 1890 and 1929 by "Lost Cause" believers and organizations like the Daughters of the Confederacy. But most of the schools named after Confederate leaders were built after 1954, over one hundred years after the Civil War—and what happened in 1954?! Yup, those schools were intentionally named in racist rebuke to the *Brown v. Board of Education* decision. The defenders of these monuments claim that they represent their "heritage," which is a euphemism for "white supremacy."

DO THE WORK

Time to take a walk! Go for stroll around your neighborhood and take note of who and what the nearby streets, schools, and buildings are named for. Who is being honored in your community—and who is being left out?

IF YOU COULD MAKE A NEW FLAG FOR YOUR COUNTRY, STATE, CITY, OR COMMUNITY, WHAT WOULD IT LOOK LIKE?

SHE DID THE WORK!

On June 27, 2015, activist Bree Newsome did the work when she scaled a 30-foot flagpole to remove a Confederate flag flying on the grounds of the South Carolina State House. Ten days earlier, nine Black churchgoers had been murdered in Charleston, SC, by a white supremacist terrorist. Newsome was arrested and the flag went back up, but her direct action made international headlines. A few weeks later, lawmakers voted to permanently remove the flag. All charges against her were dropped, and she continues to work for racial justice.

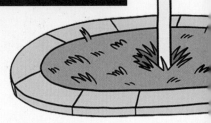

CENTERING BLACK WOMEN'S *VOICES*

Conversations about dismantling white supremacy need to center the voices of Black women, who have been speaking and writing about race, gender, struggle, and triumph for centuries. So here we are, in the center of the book. Please take some time to absorb and enjoy these voices.

ANNA JULIA COOPER
FROM *A VOICE FROM THE SOUTH* (1892)

"Only the BLACK WOMAN can say 'when and where I enter, in the quiet, undisputed dignity of my womanhood, without violence and without suing or special patronage, then and there the whole Negro race enters with me.'"

TRESSIE MCMILLAN COT
FROM *THICK* (2019)

"I am living in the most opportune time in Black hist that means, still, that I will die younger, live poorer, r violence, and be punished by social policy for being aren't true for almost any other group in this nation. Th to be Black in America and it is still that statistical

FRANCES ELLEN WATKINS HARPER
FROM HER SPEECH "WE ARE ALL BOUND UP TOGETHER" (1866)

"I do not believe that giving the woman the ballot is immediately going to cure all the ills of life. I do not believe that white women are dew-drops just exhaled from the skies....
You white women speak here of rights. I speak of wrongs....
Talk of giving women the ballot-box? Go on. I tell you that if there is any class of people who need to be lifted out of their airy nothings and selfishness, it is the white women of America."

MARY CHURCH TERRELL
FROM HER SPEECH "WHAT IT MEANS TO BE COLORED IN THE CAPITAL OF THE US" (1906)

"For fifteen years I have resided in Washington D.C., and while it was far from being a paradise for colored people when I first touched these shores it has been doing its level best ever since to make conditions for us intolerable."

ANGELA Y. DAVIS
FROM *FREEDOM IS A CONSTANT STRUGGLE* (2015)

"Sometimes we have to do the work even though we don't yet see a glimmer on the horizon that it's actually going to be possible."

JOAN MOR
FROM *WHEN CHICKENHEADS COM*

"More than any other generation b committed to 'keeping it real.' We one that samples and layers many vo the old and flips it into something n

MARIA W. STEWART
FROM HER SPEECH "WHY SIT YE HERE AND DIE?" (1832)

". . . Methinks I heard a spiritual interrogation— 'Who shall go forward, and take off the reproach that is cast upon the people of color? Shall it be a woman?'"

NTOZAKE SHANGE
FROM THE STAGE PRODUCTION *FOR COLORED GIRLS WHO HAVE CONSIDERED SUICIDE/ WHEN THE RAINBOW IS ENUF* (1976)

"but bein alive & bein a woman & bein colored is a metaphysical dilemma/ i havent conquered yet/ do you see the point my spirit is too ancient to understand the separation of soul & gender/ my love is too delicate to have thrown back on my face my love is too delicate to have thrown back on my face my love is too beautiful to have thrown back on my face my love is too sanctified to have thrown back on my face my love is too magic to have thrown back on my face my love is too saturday nite to have thrown back on my face my love is too complicated to have thrown back on my face my love is too music to have thrown back on my face"

Mia Birdsong is a family and community activist and the author of *How We Show Up*.

Marita Odette Bonner (b. 1899, Boston, MA) published her first essay, "On Being Young—a Woman—and Colored," in *The Crisis*, the journal of the NAACP that was started by W. E. B. Du Bois and edited by Jessie Redmon Fauset.

Combahee River Collective (formed 1974, Boston, MA) was a Black lesbian feminist activist organization that directly challenged the white supremacy of the women's movement.

Anna Julia Cooper (b. 1858, Raleigh, NC) was a writer, teacher, mathematician, and leading public intellectual.

Tressie McMillan Cottom (Harlem, NY) is a writer, sociologist, professor, and public scholar.

Kimberlé Crenshaw (b. 1959, Canton, OH) is a lawyer and professor, and one of the leading scholars in the field of Critical Race Theory.

Angela Y. Davis (b. 1944, Birmingham, AL) is a political activist, philosopher, professor, and an author.

Paula Giddings (b. 1947, Yonkers, NY) is a Black feminist historian and the author of numerous books about Black women's history.

Frances Ellen Watkins Harper (b. 1825, Baltimore, MD) was an accomplished poet, writer, lecturer, and abolitionist.

Lorraine Hansberry (b. 1930, Chicago, IL) was a playwright and the first Black woman to have a play (*A Raisin in the Sun*) performed on Broadway.

Zora Neale Hurston (b. 1891, Notasulga, AL) was an author, filmmaker, cultural anthropologist, and central figure during the Harlem Renaissance.

Claudia Jones (b. 1915, Trinidad and Tobago) was a journalist and radical communist, feminist, and Black nationalist activist.

Mikki Kendall (b. 1976, Chicago, IL) is an author, a cultural critic, an activist, and the author of *Hood Feminism*.

Joan Morgan (b. 1965, Jamaica) is a Jamaican-born/South Bronx–raised hip-hop journalist and cultural critic.

Rev. Pauli Murray (b. 1910, Baltimore, MD) was a civil rights lawyer and activist and the first Black American woman to be ordained as an Episcopal priest.

Ntozake Shange (b. 1948, Trenton, NJ) was a Black feminist poet and playwright best known for her acclaimed theater piece *For Colored Girls Who Have Considered Suicide / When the Rainbow Is Enuf.*

Maria W. Stewart (b. 1803, Hartford, CT) was the first American woman to deliver a public speech, and the first woman to speak before a "mixed" audience of men and women.

Mary Church Terrell (b. 1863, Memphis, TN) was an educator, suffrage activist, and one of the first Black women in America to receive a college degree.

TOM

ory in the United States and
isk more exposure to police
a Black woman in ways that
at is the best it has ever been
y bad at the macro level."

MIA BIRDSONG

FROM HER 2015 TED TALK "THE STORY WE TELL ABOUT POVERTY ISN'T TRUE"

"Let us remember what we are capable of; all that we
have built with blood, sweat, and dreams; all the cogs that
keep turning; and the people kept afloat because of our
backbreaking work. Remember that we are magic."

REV. PAULI MURRAY

"If anyone should ask
a Negro woman in
America what has been
her greatest achievement,
her honest answer would
be, 'I survived!'"
(1970)

MARITA BONNER

FROM THE ESSAY "ON BEING YOUNG—
A WOMAN—AND COLORED" (1925)

"You long to explode and hurt
everything white; friendly;
unfriendly. But you know that
you cannot live with a chip
on your shoulder even if you
can manage a smile around
your eyes—without getting
steely and brittle and
losing the softness that
makes you a woman."

ZORA NEALE HURSTON

FROM THE ESSAY "HOW IT FEELS TO BE
COLORED ME" (1928)

"Sometimes, I feel discriminated
against, but it does not make
me angry. It merely astonishes
me. How can any deny
themselves the pleasure of my
company? It's beyond me."

MIKKI KENDALL

FROM *HOOD FEMINISM* (2020)

"There's nothing feminist about
having so many resources at
your fingertips and choosing
to be ignorant. Nothing
empowering or enlightening
in deciding that intent trumps
impact. Especially when the
consequences aren't going to
be experienced by you, but
will instead be experienced by
someone from a marginalized
community...

"So how do we address that?"

GAN

E HOME TO ROOST (1999)

efore us, we need a feminism
need a voice like our music—
ces, injects its sensibilities into
w, provocative, and powerful."

PAULA GIDDINGS

"It was my mother
who gave me my voice.
She did this, I know now,
by clearing a space where
my words could fall, grow,
then find their way
to others." (1995)

CLAUDIA JONES

FROM HER ESSAY "AN END TO THE NEGLECT OF THE
PROBLEMS OF THE NEGRO WOMAN" (1949)

"Historically, the Negro woman has been
the guardian, the protector, of the Negro
family. From the days of the slave traders
down to the present, the Negro woman has
had the responsibility of caring for
the needs of the family, of militantly
shielding it from the blows of Jim
Crow insults, of reading children in an
atmosphere of lynch terror, segregation,
and police brutality, and of fighting
for an education for the children."

LORRAINE HANSBERRY

FROM THE SPEECH
"TO BE YOUNG, GIFTED,
AND BLACK" (1964)

"You are young, gifted,
and Black. In the
year 1964, I, for one,
can think of no more
dynamic combination
that a person
might be."

TELL IT LIKE IT IS By Adesina O. Koiki

The theme of this puzzle is the great **Ida B. Wells**. She leveraged her privilege as an educated journalist to investigate, document, and publicize lynchings in America. Her steadfast efforts to shed light on these crimes—which often went unreported and unpunished—were instrumental in finally raising awareness of these "Southern horrors."

ACROSS

1 Large reception area
5 Alphabetical #1 hit for the Jackson 5
8 Popular breakfast chain
9 Edible seed in a pod
10 *The Memphis Free Press and Headlight* was one … and co-owned and edited by 15-Across
13 The Mavericks, on NBA scoreboards
14 MEM (and LAX) posting
15 19th-century journalist and suffragist who was posthumously awarded a Pulitzer Prize special citation in 2020
19 "Mona Lisa" singer ___ King Cole
20 Parisian "yes"
21 With "The," 1895 pamphlet by 15-Across detailing lynchings and other racist tactics used to re-establish white supremacy post–Civil War
24 Point-earning tennis serve
25 Actress/choreographer Perez
26 "Neither" go-with
27 Parenting pair, perhaps

DOWN

1 An official language of India
2 In the lead
3 Inhabitant of an area south of Edinburgh
4 Some vinyl records, for short
5 Spotted horse breed of North America
6 Spelling competition
7 Hertz rental
11 Gray shade
12 Had brunch
16 "Break me off a piece of that Kit Kat ___"
17 Graphic in detail
18 Thanksgiving servings
21 Took part in a 5K
22 Green prefix
23 Cape ___, Massachusetts

Answers on page 156

CHAPTER

4

What Do I Dooooo?

SOMETIMES THE ENORMITY of white supremacy leaves us feeling helpless and ineffectual. But there are always places in our lives where we CAN take action—whether it's within ourselves, our home, our community, or our nation. In this chapter we practice:

➩ How to Self-Reflect

➩ How to Make Your Own Sign

➩ How to Talk to Your People

➩ How to Speak Up

➩ How to Stay in Your Lane

➩ How to Rethink Policing

➩ How to Donate Your Money

SUPPLIES

PARTNER   PEN/PENCIL   INTERNET   ART SUPPLIES

SCISSORS   TAPE   CARDBOARD

WKB: Guess what? If you've actually been reading this book and doing the activities, then you've been doing the work all along. Congratulations! You have ended racism.

KS: Just kidding.

WKB: But seriously: "Doing the work" can and does look like all kinds of things. Yes, it looks like taking to the streets to protest injustice, but it also looks like relearning histories and facing your own shit. It looks like conversations you have in private, as well as posts you make on social media.

KS: So what should you do? What should you keep doing? What should you probably not do anymore, and what can you do better?

WKB: Because all of this can be overwhelming, we've divided this chapter into four sections. We're going to dig into things you can do:

- Within yourself
- Within your home
- Within your community
- And beyond, within the nation and the world

KS: It's good to start in one area and grow into wider spheres of action so you can build your skills and not overreach. You don't want to show up on your first day of antiracist activism and start telling experienced community leaders what to do.

WKB: Seriously. Please don't do that.

KS: So without further ado, it's time for . . .

DIRECTIONS: What work are you already doing in these four categories? And what work do you want to do? Read the examples and fill in your own. Feel free to come back to this page and add ideas as they come!

SELF!

(ex: research family histories; read Angela Davis's biography; sign up for antiracist training; talk about my racist dad in therapy)

HOME!

(ex: check out diverse picture books from the library for the kids; subscribe to a Black-owned CSA; put an "END WHITE SUPREMACY" sign in window; buy beauty products from BIPOC-owned companies)

COMMUNITY!

(ex: call out racism in Nextdoor threads; volunteer at a local food bank; offer to help translate materials at my kid's school into other languages; shop at local BIPOC- and immigrant-owned businesses)

NATION + WORLD!

(ex: become recurring donor for grassroots BIPOC-led org with national efforts; donate to campaigns of progressive BIPOC and LGBTQ+ political candidates [especially if you're in a "blue state"/progressive area]; learn about the struggles of oppressed peoples in other parts of the globe)

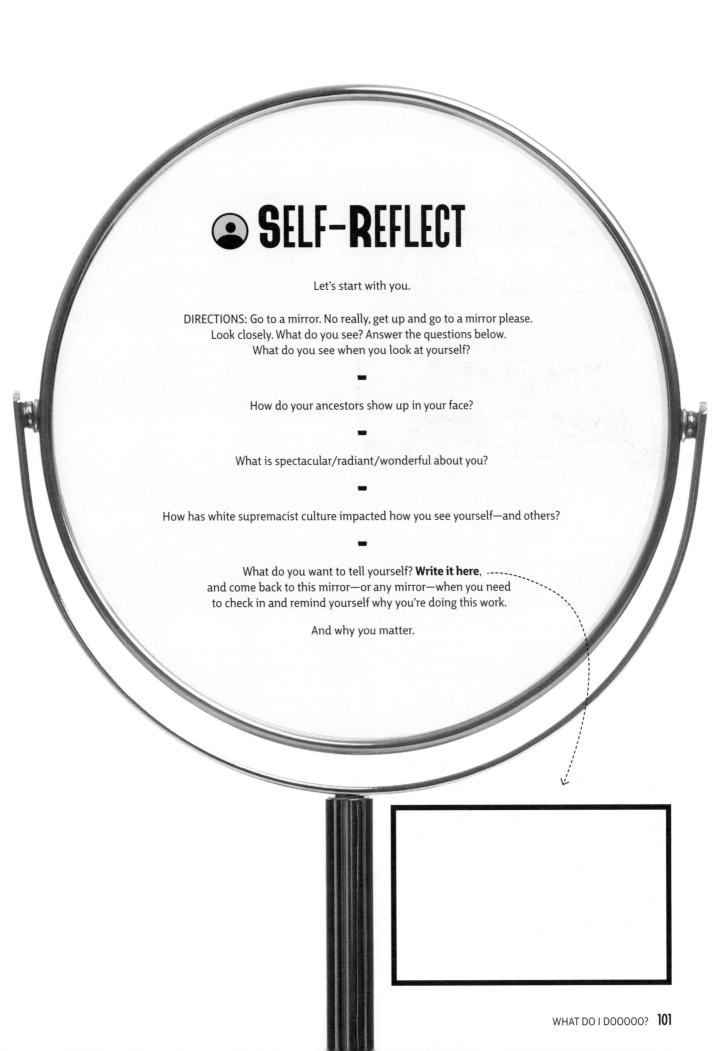

⊙ SELF-REFLECT

Let's start with you.

DIRECTIONS: Go to a mirror. No really, get up and go to a mirror please.
Look closely. What do you see? Answer the questions below.
What do you see when you look at yourself?

-

How do your ancestors show up in your face?

-

What is spectacular/radiant/wonderful about you?

-

How has white supremacist culture impacted how you see yourself—and others?

-

What do you want to tell yourself? **Write it here**, - - - -
and come back to this mirror—or any mirror—when you need
to check in and remind yourself why you're doing this work.

And why you matter.

Stay in your lane!

KS: The phrase "stay in your lane" is often kind of a dis—you might use it to tell someone to stay out of a situation they don't know much about.

WKB: Shut up and go back to your comfort zone, basically.

KS: It can definitely be useful advice.

WKB: But are lanes necessarily a bad thing?

KS: I don't think they are. We all have our own interests. We live in different places, we belong to different communities. And the big things that happen "out there" in the world often show up in smaller, localized ways within our lanes.

"Lanes" are your real-life spaces (school, house of worship, work, gym, yoga studio, book club, coffee shop, etc.) as well as virtual spaces (online communities, social media, fandoms, etc.). They're the places you go when you leave the house, and the places/groups that you give your time, energy, and attention to. And guaranteed, none of these "lanes" are untouched by white supremacy. It shows up in every damn space, taking root and thriving as long as it goes unchecked.

Your lanes are also places where you often have more power and influence than you think.

WKB: It's easy to look at the world and say, "I want to end racism!" It's harder to look at your own neighbors and tell them that the MAGA sticker on their truck makes you feel unsafe.

KS: Right. When the cops shoot an unarmed Black man in another state, you can say, "Things are really messed up with the police there!" But what about the police in your own community? What's going on right there, where you live?

WKB: And if your response is something like, "Well, that doesn't happen here . . ." I just want to make sure you've actually spoken to an actual Black, Latino/a, or Indigenous person who lives there. Because they miiiiiiiiiiiiiiight have a different response.

KS: Often when people without a lot of activist experience want to figure out what to do there's a sense that it has to be this huge deal, like you have to transform into some superhero who organizes a massive protest and starts a nonprofit and hosts a charity auction all at once.

WKB: Or another podcast! What we really need is more podcasts.

KS: Figuring out your lanes can also prevent you from spreading yourself too thin. Sometimes your lane is the thing right in front of you. Your workplace, your book club, the PTA.

WKB: As in the "Parent Teacher Association"?

KS: I have a story: The PTA never occurred to me as a site of activism, but a few years ago my friend Sia convinced me otherwise. Sia, a Black single mom who's no longer with us, was a lifelong activist. We were talking about pushing for racial justice in our community, and Sia insisted that our friend Leslie run for PTA president. We were surprised. Isn't the PTA just bake sales and boring meetings? Sia was like, yes, but also, nah. This needs to be your shit, she said. Step up and help those babies, get those white moms talking about equity. So Leslie did it: She led that public school PTA for two years. It didn't always look like "activism," she says, but she pushed the parents and school community in new directions around racial justice and equity, and she did some great work.

WKB: So let's figure out our lanes. When I really think about it, I have a lot.

KS: Me too. Let's each choose one.

WKB: I'm thinking my kids' school, my neighborhood, my Twitterverse, the stand-up comedy world. For this exercise, I'll do showbiz!

KS: There's no business like it!

KAMAU'S LANE

WHAT'S MY LANE?

Showbiz!

WHO ELSE IS IN IT?

Kim Kardashian, Dwayne "The Rock" Johnson, Chris Evans, a bunch of other Chrises. Since 2011, I've worked in TV production with network executives, producers, writers, directors, and editors. Since I work at CNN, my lane includes many journalists, too.

WHAT'S MY ROLE?
WHAT ARE MY SKILLS?

I'm a producer, writer, director, and on-screen talent. I'm often one of the people leading a team. I'm good at listening to and talking with people. I'm good at helping people have challenging conversations.

HOW DOES WHITE SUPREMACY SHOW UP?

High-level leadership in showbiz is still really white. I'm regularly in meetings with executives where I'm the only Black person or person of color in the meeting. Even though I have the title of executive producer, I often have to fight to be treated like one. Sometimes white collaborators don't trust my expertise about Black things. Showbiz also has a problem with not prioritizing off-camera diversity. Even if there are Black actors or Black subject matter on-screen, sometimes it doesn't feel Black because there aren't enough Black people working behind the scenes.

WHAT'S BEING DONE ABOUT IT?

Some networks and production companies have made big investments in BIPOC creatives like Issa Rae, Ryan Coogler, Ava DuVernay, and Mindy Kaling so they can create even more content. Respected activists and organizations like Color of Change and Culture Strike are getting hired to consult on projects.

WHAT'S THE FIRST STEP?

The first step is knowing what you're willing to do to make things different. When I first got access to the showbiz lane with a TV show called *Totally Biased*, I hired friends of mine who would have been passed up for writing and on-camera jobs on other shows. During the first season of *United Shades of America* I was the only person of color in a leadership role. I decided I wouldn't go back for a second season if they didn't hire a more diverse team. And they did.

WHAT CAN I DO ABOUT IT?

In addition to trying to get more diverse talent into leadership positions and more diverse stories on-screen, I'm trying to mentor the people I bring on board. I know how treacherous showbiz is for people who aren't white cis men. I'm also trying to raise the quality of my own work and the quality I demand from my teams.

 # GET TO KNOW YOUR LANE

DIRECTIONS: List as many of your "lanes" as you can think of in the space below. Then choose TWO of those, and complete the activity.

What's my lane?

Who else is in it?

**What's my role?
What are my skills?**

How does white supremacy show up?

What's my lane?

Who else is in it?

**What's my role?
What are my skills?**

How does white supremacy show up?

What can I do about it?

What's the first step?

What's being done about it?

What can I do about it?

What's the first step?

What's being done about it?

SHE DID THE WORK!

Septima Clark is a powerful example of someone who saw a way to use one of her lanes—her job as a schoolteacher—to make a huge impact on the civil rights movement.

Born in South Carolina in 1898, she began her teaching career in an all-Black school on an island off the coast of South Carolina since Black teachers weren't allowed to work in Charleston. She taught adult literacy classes at night and created a curriculum that encouraged folks to write about their lives. She believed that education was the key to political power, and said that "literacy is liberation." She became a director at the Highlander Folk School, where she developed the Citizenship Schools, a grassroots education program that would help Black folks learn to read so that they could pass literacy tests and register to vote. She wanted to empower people to know their rights and to see themselves as full, worthy citizens.

By 1961, there were 37 Citizenship Schools. Clark then partnered with the Southern Christian Leadership Conference (SCLC), becoming the director of education and teaching, and traveling around the South to train teachers and establish more Citizenship School programs. The classes she established schooled thousands of Black Americans on basic literacy and civics. She became known as the "Mother of the Movement."

🏠 MAKE YOUR OWN SIGN!

One action you can take in your home is to show your support for a cause, an issue, or a candidate by displaying a visible sign.

Depending on where you live and who you are, this may or may not seem like a big deal. We gave you an "END WHITE SUPREMACY" sign at the beginning of the book, and reminded you that putting up a sign is just one part of doing the work. But in some communities, a sign can mark you as a target, and aligning yourself with a cause or candidate can be a risky act.

We know this—and we ask you to be brave. Be public! Show your community what side you're on.

🧻 LET'S MAKE A SIGN!

What do the people in your home care about? When people walk past your home, or come to visit, what values and beliefs do you want to make visible? Your sign can be a general statement that reflects your beliefs, or a message in response to a current situation.

STEP **1** **FIND YOUR SIGN MATERIAL.**

- Cardboard. It's a great way to repurpose cardboard delivery boxes!

- Poster board. One left over from the science fair?

- A piece of paper. Literally, just a piece of paper. Colored construction paper, white printer paper, the backside of your kid's old math worksheet—anything works.

STEP **2** **DECIDE WHAT TO WRITE.**

- Keep your message simple and clear.

- If you want to add a web address or hashtag so people can learn more, go for it. If you're super tech-savvy you can even print out a QR code!

- If you're stuck, go online—you'll find plenty of people sharing clever protest signs.

STEP **3** MAKE THE SIGN.

- Make your letters bold so your message can be seen from a distance.
- Sharpies are great, as are regular markers.
- Wanna be fancy? Make it colorful—add glitter if that's your thing.
- Don't wanna be fancy? Fine.
- Got kids? Make it a family project. Let them write the words if they know how, and let little ones add drawings and doodles.

STEP **4** DISPLAY THE SIGN.

- Decide how visible you want the sign to be and where it should go.
- If you're displaying it outside, consider whether you need to keep the sign protected—will it be ruined by rain or snow? Do you live in an area where people might take or deface the sign?

⌂ Talk to Your People

"How do I talk to my _____ about racism?"

(A) Uncle who tells racist jokes at family gatherings.

(B) Colleague who complained that "white men won't get promotions anymore" after the DEI seminar.

(C) Friend who "totally believes in equality but just wishes people didn't have to be so angry about it all the time."

(D) Neighbor who still has the "TRUMP" lawn sign up.

(E) High school friend who's not like *racist* racist, but keeps mentioning Black-on-Black crime.

(F) Liberal aunt who "marched in the '60s!" but is very angry when protesters break windows.

(G) All of the above. *Whew.*

KS: We hear variations on this theme often, especially from white people who are trying to figure out how to talk to the white people in their lives who don't get it. Who don't want to get it. Or who "get it" when it's convenient for them, but bristle at "the radical stuff."

WKB: First thing: We're glad you're asking this question. Good job. Keep going. This is the work.

KS: Unfortunately, there's no one magic answer or one easy way to have these conversations.

WKB: Also! This isn't just for white people. There are plenty of ways that we can internalize the lies told and taught to us about our own communities (see: Ben Carson, Elaine Chao, Ted Cruz, et al). It's even easier to internalize lies we're told and taught about communities that are not our own. Some of these conversations need to happen between people who are not white, but who are still upholding white supremacy in various ways.

> "But … it'll be awkward."
> "But … I don't know what to say."
> "But … I'm not like an expert."
> "But … I don't want to get into a huge fight."
> "But … will it even change anything?"

KS: Hard? Yes. Awkward? Probably. Productive? We can't guarantee that. But does it need to happen?

WKB: We're gonna go with yes, yes it does. You can't always predict how and when these conversations are going to happen, but it's still helpful to be prepared.

BEFORE
THE CONVERSATION…

Consider your relationship to this person.
How long have you known them? How often are you in contact? And what are you willing to risk—and possibly lose—if the conversation doesn't go well? The way you approach a family member will be different from the way you approach a colleague. Be clear on what's at stake in the relationship.

Know your goals.
Do you need to confront this person about a very specific action or behavior, or is it a more general concern?

Be prepared.
Look up *"how to talk to people about racism"* and read not one but many of the articles that come up. Take notes.

Know where you stand.
Confidence in your own thoughts and opinions can help you stay grounded during challenging conversations.

Know your facts.
You don't have to be *"an expert,"* but it can help to be prepared with "hard evidence" to back up your beliefs. That said, "facts" won't necessarily change hearts and minds—most people prefer to feel listened to, not lectured at.

Meet people where they are.
Think about where they're coming from, and why they might be thinking/acting the way they do.

Acknowledge their beliefs and value, and aim to build on them, rather than trying to fundamentally change them. Even if you disagree, can you find a place of understanding and some things you do agree on?

Have boundaries. If you don't feel safe with a face-to-face conversation, consider other modes of communication. Write an email or a letter. There's always Zoom!

Beware of Facebook! Repeat after us: "A social media comment thread is not a space for productive dialogue." See a post or comment you want to address? Take the conversation to DMs.

DURING

THE CONVERSATION ...

Get consent.
Ask the person if they're open to having a conversation about the topic (even if the conversation has already started). Just say *"Hey, I know we don't see eye-to-eye on this, but I'm cool to keep talking if you are."* This reframes it as a bigger discussion.

Ask questions.
This bears repeating: ASK QUESTIONS. You don't have to do all the talking, or the explaining. And very few people—possibly zero people—like to be told what they should do or think or believe.

 LISTEN.
This is a hard one for most of us, but it's where the rubber meets the road. Listen to actually understand. If someone's talking and they sense that you're just waiting for them to be done so you can say your piece, it can shut down dialogue.

Repeat their words back to them, especially if what they've said is hard for you to understand/accept. Rephrase their talking points, and ask if you've heard them correctly.

Stick to things you can prove—don't get bogged down or lost in "unprovable" scenarios (even if you believe them to be obvious or true).

Notice your body.
Holding your breath? Clenching your jaw? Balling your fists and wanting to swing?
It's OK to take a break and to walk away if the conversation feels hurtful or too heated.

It's not one-and-done.
This ABSOLUTELY won't be a one-time thing. A single conversation has never led to a major breakthrough. Name one time that has happened. We'll wait.... Nope, not even then. Prepare the follow-up, and keep the conversation going.

High five! Did you find common ground? Learn from each other? Acknowledge the things you each did well in the conversation.

AFTER

THE CONVERSATION ...

What worked? What can you build on, and what might you do differently next time?

Follow up. If you offered resources or references during the conversation, remember to send those.

Next steps. How will you proceed? Do you need to do more research? Rethink your approach? Send a text and ask when they can talk again?

Take care of yourself. It's OK to feel angry, hurt, or unsure about how to proceed. If you need help processing anything that came up during the conversation, reach out to your friends (like your accountability partner!). Talking to others who've experienced similar situations can be super helpful.

If it feels right, reach out. Let them know what you appreciated about the conversation, and, if applicable, what you learned from listening to them.

Give yourself credit for doing something important.

> Now you have some strategies for having hard conversations, and planning in advance for impactful dialogue. But what about those moments where it just happens?

THIS IS A PARTNER ACTIVITY

WKB: There you are, enjoying a cold beer with your old pal Mike, when all of the sudden he opens his mouth and—

KS: I think most of us have been caught off guard by someone's casual (or not-so-casual) racism, and regretted not speaking up in the moment.

WKB: There's nothing quite like the hindsight of I-should've-said-that-to-the-racist. You replay the moment over and over, crafting the perfect comeback. Truth is, it can be hard to do it in the moment.

KS: Is it weird to practice having conversations with racists?

WKB: I mean, at this point in America, we gotta try everything.

KS: Great! Ready to do some improv?

WKB: You know the rule! The answer to that is: Yes!

We didn't want to generate new racist comments for people to read out loud when there are plenty of existing examples to draw from. We borrowed some actual racist bullshit said by actual high-profile individuals, and put them in imaginary scenes so you can improvise.

And if you ever end up in a conversation with Tucker Carlson, tell him Kamau says . . . nevermind. Not in this book.

HOW TO SPEAK UP

DIRECTIONS:

⇨ Get a scene partner.

⇨ Read the scene on your own first. Think about how you'll respond, but don't discuss with each other in advance.

⇨ Run through the scene at least three times. Try out different responses, tones, and approaches.

⇨ Switch roles and let your scene partner be the responder.

⇨ Move on to the next scene.

```
DO THE WORK: How to Speak Up 1.
Writer's Draft 05/02/21

          Scene 1: The One about America


INT. YOUR KITCHEN -- AFTERNOON


You sit at the counter, phone to your ear.


               YOU
    Hey, I'm not sure if I'm going to come to
    the 4th of July BBQ this year . . .


INT. HIS LIVING ROOM -- CONTINUOUS


He reclines in his La-Z-Boy, drink in hand.


               HIM
    What? You come every year.


               YOU
    Honestly, with everything going on in the
    world . . . I'm not feeling proud of America
    right now.

               HIM
    We birthed a nation from nothing! I mean,
    there was nothing here. I mean, yes we
    have Native Americans, but candidly there
    isn't much Native American culture in
    American culture.*


               YOU
    [Finish the scene . . . ]

                              *RICK SANTORUM, 2021
```

SCENE 2: The One about Soccer

EXT. SOCCER FIELD -- AFTERNOON

Parents stand along the sidelines of a middle-
school soccer game. You hold a tray of orange slices
and a DAD approaches.

                    DAD
              Great game, huh?

                    YOU
Yeah, these kids are great. Your son's really got
some skills!

                    DAD
Thanks. Pretty fast for a white kid, huh?

                    YOU
              (Unsure) Yeah.

                    DAD
Sorry to get all "racial." This stuff just drives
me crazy, ya know?

                    YOU
              Which stuff?

                    DAD
I mean.... White nationalist, white supremacist,
Western civilization — how did that language become
offensive?*

                    YOU
[Finish the scene...]

                         *REP. STEVE KING, 2016

SCENE 3:
The One about the Coworker

INT. BREAKROOM AT WORK -- MIDDAY

YOU enter to find colleagues
seated around the table eating
lunch. As you grab your meal
from the fridge, you overhear
a COLLEAGUE talking loudly
while others eat their salads.

              COLLEAGUE
So like I was saying, everybody
knows that Barack Obama would
still be in the state Senate in
Illinois if he were white.*

                    YOU
[Finish the scene...]

              *TUCKER CARLSON, 2008

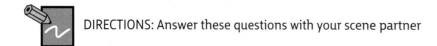 DIRECTIONS: Answer these questions with your scene partner

THIS IS A
PARTNER ACTIVITY

WHAT ARE SOME STRATEGIES YOU USED WHEN YOU WERE THE PERSON RESPONDING TO RACIST STATEMENTS THAT YOU'D LIKE TO TRY OUT IN THE REAL WORLD SOMETIME?

Partner A

Partner B

WHAT'S SOMETHING GREAT THAT YOUR SCENE PARTNER DID WHEN THEY WERE THE ONE RESPONDING TO RACIST STATEMENTS?

Partner A

Partner B

WHAT SURPRISED YOU ABOUT HOW YOU FELT, THOUGHT, OR BEHAVED IN THESE SCENES?

Partner A

Partner B

DELEGATE

When you delegate, you choose to get someone else involved.

EXCUSE ME! CAN WE PLEASE GET A MANAGER OVER HERE?

DOCUMENT

Document the interaction by taking photos or a video. If safe/appropriate, approach the person to see if you can send footage to them or their family. If not, save footage in case it's needed later.

DELAY

When you delay, you take time to communicate with the person who was harassed. You may not have been able to disrupt the harassment, but you can care for the person.

WE JUST SAW WHAT HAPPENED. DO YOU NEED HELP? CAN WE SIT WITH YOU FOR A MINUTE?

DO THE WORK

- Sign yourself up for a bystander training.
- If you're a parent, sign your kids up for training and/or share what you learn.
- Consider bringing a bystander training program into your workplace, community, or organizations you're part of.
- Turn to the end of the book to fill out your Upstander Commitment Card!

SAFETY MATTERS!

There are circumstances (in public and in private) where intervention might escalate a situation and lead to physical harm for you and/or others involved. There might be times when you don't have the skills or resources to handle a situation. And your identity/physical ability might limit your capacity to safely intervene. If you witness a situation and know you can't safely intervene, there are still ways to monitor from a distance, support the person who was harmed, document the event, and/or provide an eyewitness account after the fact.

> Now let's talk about the fact that people really need to stop calling the damn cops about things they really don't need to call the damn cops about.

KS: Hear, hear! When we learn to be upstanders, we can feel more empowered to handle crises in our communities without involving the police.

WKB: How about a pop quiz!

KS: You mean a cop quiz?

WKB: Ahem. Who's the comedian here?

Q: Between 2010 and 2020. what percentage of calls placed to the LAPD were about violent crime?

40%	8%
22%	57%

A: 8 PERCENT. Only 8 percent of calls to the LAPD over that ten-year period were for violent crimes.

The percentage of violent crime calls in cities like New Haven, CT; New Orleans, LA; and Oakland, CA, where I live? 4 percent. And yet here in Oakland, around 42 percent of our general fund goes to police. By now we should have all seen enough videos of seemingly simple interactions with police turning deadly to know that police spend a lot of time doing things they're not really trained (or needed) to do, including responding to people with mental health issues, managing minor disputes, and issuing traffic citations. People have been murdered by police in all of those situations.

KS: Sometimes I feel like we're all in a long-term abusive relationship with the police. No matter how many times the cops reveal themselves to be bastions of white supremacist, misogynist violence, we keep coming back to them. We're trained from birth to believe that an armed police force is the only way to maintain safety and security in our communities. Uh, Kamau, do you have any thoughts?

WKB: No, you're doing great, actually. Continue . . .

KS: We've trained generation after generation of humans to see Black bodies (and Latino/a and Indigenous bodies) as criminals—even cops of color get this messaging. We get this messaging, and believe we need protection. And since we see police as our only option, we accept and rationalize behaviors that in any other context would cause national outrage.

WKB: Go on.

KS: What if every few months (or weeks, or days) the news reported that police have murdered an unarmed person who looks not like you, Kamau, but like me. A blond white mom. Imagine if blond white moms were getting pulled over for broken taillights on our minivans, and then getting shot to death with our children in the car because we didn't listen to the cops/reached for our purses too quickly/resisted arrest/asked too many questions/didn't smile big enough.

WKB: England would probably invade us and make us a colony again.

KS: Imagine that happening, and imagine STILL being told that the police are there to protect us all.

WKB: I don't even have to imagine how that would feel because I literally know exactly how that feels.

KS: So what do we do?

WKB: Don't ask me. You're the one on a roll here!

KS: I'm still learning, especially from activists and organizers who've spent decades advocating for the complete abolition of police and prisons. That's a vision I support—but we're obviously nowhere near that.

One of the most impactful things we can do is to think critically about our personal relationship to policing and community safety. When and why have you called the police before? What happens when you call the police? Does a person experiencing a mental health crisis need help from people trained to shoot and arrest, or people trained to de-escalate and care? If your life is in danger, you'll call 911. But for other non-emergency situations, ask yourself: *Do I need people to show up with guns? Is there another way to resolve this? Who else can I call?*

WKB: While you're asking yourself questions, here's a few more: Are you trying to "police" someone when that's not your job? Have you ever had a negative encounter with police? Have you ever had a positive encounter with police? Do you believe there's an epidemic of police violence in the Black, Latino/a, and Indigenous communities? Why or why not? Do you live in a "safe" neighborhood? Who's it "safe" for? What does safety mean? What are police for? Who and what do they protect?

KS: And what does a world without police look like?

SHE DID THE WORK!

Darnella Frazier did the work on May 25, 2020, when she observed a conflict between a white police officer and a Black man outside of a convenience store in Minneapolis, MN. Darnella, a 17-year-old high school student, had taken her younger cousin to the store to get snacks. She quickly ushered her cousin into the store to keep her away from the altercation—and then came back outside to hold up her phone and press record. Darnella's video captured the 9 minutes and 29 seconds that officer Derek Chauvin kneeled on the neck of George Floyd. It captured the many passersby who attempted to be upstanders and intervene in the unnecessary violence. It captured Floyd's death, and after she uploaded it to Facebook, it was viewed millions of times by horrified people around the world. Her video became the "star witness" in the prosecution of Derek Chauvin, who was found guilty on three counts by a jury in April 2021, making him one of the very few cops ever convicted of murder.

BEFORE YOU CALL THE POLICE, ASK YOURSELF:

Is this a situation that should concern me?
⇨ Yeah, someone actually needs help.
⇨ No, I should relax and mind my business.

Is this situation an inconvenience that I can deal with?
⇨ Yeah, it's annoying but I can deal.
⇨ No, it needs a response.

Can I handle it on my own? Can I talk to the person?
⇨ Yes, I can try to talk to them.
⇨ No way, I need help.

Is there someone nearby who can help me? Can I call a neighbor or a friend?
⇨ I can try.
⇨ No, this situation needs a professional.

Is there a nonpolice resource I can call? A mental health crisis line? The fire department? A local non-emergency number? A domestic violence crisis hotline?
⇨ Yes! I have those saved in my phone. I'll try that.
⇨ NO. I'm calling the cops.

If I call the cops, do I understand that once they arrive I cannot control what they do? Do I understand the impact of this decision?

Evolution of Policing

The crisis in American policing isn't new at all. The police system has always been anti-Black, because that is how it was designed. As the saying goes: "It's not a bug—it's a feature." From slave patrols to militias to watchmen to the development of the first American police forces in the 1830s, the function of American policing is rooted in two things: controlling the movement of enslaved (and later, immigrant) populations and protecting the property of rich white people. The look and feel has changed over time, but the song has remained pretty much the same....

5 THINGS YOU NEED TO KNOW ABOUT . . .

We asked **Nikki Jones**, professor of African American Studies at UC Berkeley, to give us a quick lesson on five things she wants everyone to know about the history of policing in America.

1 The American police system can be traced back to the Barbados Slave Codes of 1661, which informed and structured a vast network of racially charged surveillance and punishment that included overseers on plantations, slave patrols around plantations, slave catchers, and ordinary white people who policed the freedom and mobility of Black people.

2 Black people have been warning other Black people to avoid the police for (at least!) 170 years. An 1851 broadside contains this warning: "Caution! COLORED PEOPLE OF BOSTON, ONE & ALL, You are hereby respectfully cautioned and advised, to avoid conversing with the Watchmen and Police Officers of Boston." Why? Police officers were "kidnapping and catching" Black people fleeing slavery and returning them to bondage.

3 The Kerner Report (1968) said that the cause of more than 160 urban uprisings in the 1960s was white racism and racist policing. In testimony to the Kerner Commission, policing scholar Albert Reiss Jr. described the "extreme racial prejudice" of law enforcement this way: "What do I mean by extreme racial prejudice? I mean that [the police] describe Negroes in terms that are not people terms. They describe them in terms of the animal kingdom."

4 After the acquittal of LAPD officers in the beating of Rodney King in 1992, it was reported that officers patrolling Black areas routinely used the term "NHI"— no humans involved—as a shorthand for crimes involving Black people.

5 In 2006, the FBI warned that policing was becoming a sought-after job for white nationalists.

TO CALL OR NOT TO CALL

Read each scenario and think about how you would react. Then choose from the options.

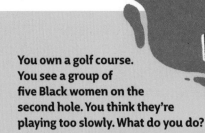

You're walking your dog in the park and you see a Black man. He asks you to put your dog on a leash, which is the law. What do you do?

(A) You put your dog on the leash.

(B) You ignore him and keep walking your dog. After all who is this guy? The leash police?

(C) You threaten to call the cops. You even pull out your phone to pretend to call the cops.

(D) CALL THE COPS!

Answer: We hope for A. We accept B. But we got some combination of C and D when white lady Amy Cooper came across Christian Cooper (no relation) in Central Park in New York City. She threatened to, and eventually did, call the police. Luckily for Christian, he recorded the interaction. And even luckier for him, the police didn't come. Amy was charged with filing a false report. Luckily for her, the charge was dropped after she completed a therapy program on racial bias. Just kidding! That wasn't luck—that was the system of white supremacy protecting a white woman.

You own a golf course. You see a group of five Black women on the second hole. You think they're playing too slowly. What do you do?

(A) Nothing.

(B) Ask the group of white men behind them if the Black women's pace of play is bothering them.

(C) Confront them about their play.

(D) CALL THE COPS! When the dispatcher asks you if one of the Black women has a weapon, respond, "Other than her mouth, there's not any weapons."

Answer: First of all, good for you for owning a golf course. We didn't know you had it like that. Daaaaaamn! In 2018, Steve Chronister, the owner of York, Pennsylvania's Grandview Golf Course, chose C. And after the women didn't immediately do exactly what he said, he went for D, calling the police twice (since they didn't come the first time). Myneca Ojo, Sandra Thompson, Karen Crosby, Sandra Harrison, and Carolyn Dow were quite literally guilty of nothing, except maybe being the only Black people playing that day. Luckily the police realized how absurd the calls were, and the women didn't end up arrested—or dead.

You're walking through a park with your partner. You see a Latino man sitting on a park bench, holding something. It might be a gun? What do you do?

(A) Keep walking.

(B) Scream "HE HAS A GUN!" and run away in a panic.

(C) CALL THE COPS!

You see an individual who appears to be a young man in a park carrying what looks to be a toy gun. You live in an open carry state. What do you do?

(A) Let the kid go on his way. He looks like a kid with a toy gun in a park.

(B) Call the police, and clearly specify that the gun is "probably fake," and that it's "probably a juvenile."

(C) JUST HURRY UP AND CALL THE COPS! YOU DON'T KNOW FOR SURE THAT IT IS A TOY GUN!

Answer: Tamir Rice was 12 years old when someone chose B (and C) and called the cops on him for "waving around" a toy gun in a park in Cleveland, OH. Though that person stated that it was likely not a real gun the dispatcher failed to relay that to the police. When you call the police, you have no control over who will show up, or how they'll react— even if you try to explain the circumstances. The officer who showed up jumped out of his still-moving car and shot Tamir within two seconds, killing him instantly.

You see a young Black man dancing down the street. What do you do?

(A) I don't understand the question. WHY WOULD THIS BE A QUESTION?

(B) Call the cops, and specify that although he looks "sketchy," no one is in danger and you don't think he is armed.

Answer: Option A is it. What's wrong with someone dancing down the street? Life is hard. Let people have some joy. Then there's B. Do you really need to call the cops for shit like this? In 2019, someone decided yes. And even though they specified that the dancer wasn't causing harm, 23-year-old Elijah McClain ended up dead. Elijah described himself as "different"—the kind of person who played violins for cats in shelters. He was bopping down the street wearing headphones and a ski mask (he often got cold). The cops who showed up escalated the situation by detaining Elijah and putting him in a choke hold. When Elijah panicked, the cops told a paramedic to sedate him by injecting him with ketamine. The dose was too strong, and Elijah went into cardiac arrest. This innocent young man was dead three days later.

Answer: A is a great answer. If you're not feeing safe, walk away. B is not a good idea. And you guessed it: The real-life answer was C. In 2014, Alex Nieto was sitting on a park bench in San Francisco, CA. He was, by several accounts, eating a burrito. And he was carrying a Taser— not a gun—because he worked as a security guard for a nightclub. The two men who saw him claimed that he had a gun when they called 911. The police showed up, confronted him, and the four cops fired a total of 59 shots at Alex, killing him. Again: Alex did not have a gun.

DO THE WORK

Learn about your local resources and options so that if you're faced with a crisis you know who to call. This includes:

- Suicide hotline
- Mental health crisis services
- Services for unhoused people
- Domestic violence crisis services
- Services for runaways/unhoused youth
- LGBTQ+ crisis support services

Save your local non-emergency numbers in your phone, including the fire department.

Turn to the end of the book to fill out a handy wallet card so you can reference those numbers easily.

If you have kids, and you teach them about calling 911 in an emergency, also teach them about when and how to call the non-emergency numbers.

Know your neighbors: Introduce yourself to them, and if people are willing, create and share a neighborhood contact list. Start a Google group or email list so neighbors can communicate and support each other.

Are you an…ally?
A co-conspirator?
An accomplice?
Someone who gives a shit but isn't familiar with any of those terms?

KS: It can be helpful to understand these terms—but what really matters is what you do, not what you "are."

WKB: Think of an ally as someone who watches the game, applauding from the bleachers. They cheer from a safe distance, maybe even waving a flag and wearing a T-shirt. Accomplices and co-conspirators? They get on the field, and play the game. Even if they're not that great at it. They might get dirty, bruised, and beat-up. They might not win. They might sit on the sidelines the whole time and not end up playing! In the end, they're willing to put themselves out there and have skin in the game.

KS: Some might argue that the latter is the more "important" work, but we think that it takes all kinds. We need people getting down and dirty on the field, but that work is not for everyone. And those people cheering in the stands help the folks on the field keep going. In her book *We Want To Do More Than Survive: Abolitionist Teaching and the Pursuit of Educational Freedom*, Dr. Bettina L. Love writes that "A co-conspirator says, 'I know the terms; I know what white privilege and white supremacy mean; now, what risks am I willing to take?' It's saying, 'I'm going to put my privilege on the line for somebody.'"

WKB: Most importantly, you're not an ally or a co-conspirator or an accomplice because you say you are. You're an ally/co-conspirator/accomplice when you show up for a marginalized individual or community and they feel supported, heard, and seen. That is solidarity. And as Alicia Garza, principal and founder of Black Futures Lab, often says: "Solidarity is a verb."

  # SKIN IN THE GAME

DIRECTIONS: Below are eight individuals who've shown us what solidarity can look like. Match the person to the description and learn about some historic heroes.

1 LARRY ITLIONG

2 RALPH LAZO

3 ANNE BRADEN

4 VIOLA LIUZZO

5 BRAD LOMAX

6 BARBARA HENRY

7 YURI KOCHIYAMA

8 GRACE LEE BOGGS

Answers on page 155

A

A white educator from Boston who was the only teacher willing to teach a Black child when her school in Louisiana was integrated in 1960. Her colleagues refused to, but she showed up every day to teach one student: six-year-old Ruby Bridges. She was ostracized by the white folks in town, but remained committed to teaching Ruby and keeping her safe.

B

A white mother of five who heeded Dr. King's call for Northerners to join the fight for civil rights after Bloody Sunday. In 1965, she drove alone from Michigan to Alabama. She marched and organized for a month until she was murdered by a KKK member while driving with a Black man from Montgomery back to Selma. The only white woman killed during the civil rights movement.

C

A Chinese American activist who built multiracial working-class coalitions and trained community organizers. She was so involved in Detroit's Black Power movement that her FBI file noted she was "probably Afro Chinese"—they couldn't understand why a Chinese woman would be so committed to another community's struggle.

D

A Mexican American teenager who was outraged that his Japanese American friends were being forced from their homes and sent to prison camps in 1942—so he decided to go with them. He boarded a train to Manzanar, and spent two years as the only known non-Japanese person to be willingly incarcerated. He spent his life working for reparations for the Japanese American community.

E

A Filipino farmworker who led a 1965 strike of over 2,000 Filipino vineyard workers. He knew the real power lay in solidarity: Filipino and Mexican workers got pitted against each other by white growers, so he convinced Cesar Chavez and his union of Mexican farmworkers to join them. He did, and they became the powerful United Farm Workers.

F

A white Southern woman who made headlines in 1954 when she purchased a home for a Black couple in a white suburb of Louisville, Kentucky. The house was bombed when neighbors realized the residents were Black. No one was charged for the attack, but she was charged with sedition and put on trial. She remained committed to racial and economic justice for life.

G

A Japanese American woman who began her antiracist work after being released from internment and moving to Harlem with her family. A mother of six, she worked with diverse neighbors on social justice causes. She invited her friend Malcolm X to her home to speak to survivors of the Hiroshima atomic bomb. She was with him when he was murdered, and an iconic photo shows her cradling his head moments after he was shot. Their unlikely friendship transcended race and gender and shaped her radical activism for decades.

H

A Black Panther organizer, and leader in the Disability Rights movement. In 1977, he helped lead over 100 disabled activists in the "504 Sit-In," America's longest peaceful occupation of a federal building. He rallied his Black Panther comrades to provide hot meals for the protesters every day. When he and 25 of the protesters flew to Washington, DC, to pressure Congress, the Panthers paid their way.

WHO Represents YOU

REPRESENTATION MATTERS!

DIRECTIONS: Fill in the information for all of your elected officials.

Electoral politics aren't the end-all-be-all of change-making, but they are an important part of the process. But first you gotta know who has been elected to represent you at all levels of government.

As their constituent, you have the right to be heard. You can make phone calls, send emails, and request meetings. You can speak at public meetings. You can propose, draft, and even introduce legislation and ballot measures.

But to do any of that, you need to know who to talk to—and how to contact them.

FLIP TO THE BACK OF THE BOOK FOR A VERSION TO HANG ON YOUR FRIDGE!

QUICK REVIEW!
The federal government has three branches: executive (the president), judicial (the Supreme Court), and legislative (Congress), which has two "bodies," aka the Senate and the House of Representatives).

Every state has two Senators, no matter its size or population. Senators serve six-year terms. State Representatives serve in the House for two-year terms, and the number of Reps is based on a state's Congressional districts, which are redrawn every 10 years.

Finally, every state is divided into counties and municipalities (cities, townships, boroughs, etc.), all of which have elected officials.

FEDERAL The two senators for my state are:

_____

Phone: _____

Email: _____ Next election: _____

_____

Phone: _____

Email: _____ Next election: _____

I live in Congressional District _____ ,

and my elected Rep is _____.

Phone: _____

Email: _____ Next election: _____

STATE

The Governor of my state is _____

Phone: _____

Email: _____ Next election: _____

The Attorney General is _____,
and my Legislative Reps are _____
_____

Phone: _____

Email: _____ Next election: _____

LOCAL

Since local government structures vary, fill in the ones you're most likely to want to contact!

_____

_____

_____

If I ever ran for elected office, I would run for

_____

because _____

_____

_____

Diversify Your Feed

When we say "your feed" we're not just talking about social media, but *all* the content you consume. The books, the TV shows and movies, the podcasts and music, and, yes, who and what you follow on the socials. It's all the information and entertainment that feeds your brain.

And when we say "diversify" we don't just mean "read one book by a Black author" or "watch a documentary about the civil rights movement" (though both of those are good ideas). We want you to take stock of your feed and consider how you can expand the perspectives you're consuming. Whose stories do you read, watch, and listen to? Whose voices are loudest, and what are they telling you about the world? Whose voices are *not* showing up in your feed, and why does that matter? In the words of the author and screenwriter Tananarive Due: "'Diversity' should just be called 'reality.' Your books, your TV shows, your movies, your articles, your curricula, need to reflect *reality*."

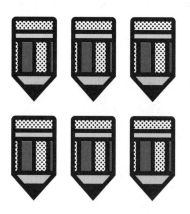

The number of Black writers in 2019 that had *New York Times* **bestselling books in any category**.

Out of 362 movies made in 2017, **only 14 had at least one Black lead role.**

8

Number of BIPOC actors in the main cast of 200 TV shows on 10 different networks

Podcasts are often seen as one of the most diverse media formats—**yet the Top 100 podcasts are overwhelmingly hosted by white men.**

Percentage of Indigenous characters depicted out of 3,134 children's books. 5 percent depicted Latino/a characters. 7 percent had AAPI characters.

Less than 6 percent of the writers, directors, and producers of US-produced films are Black. In some genres (like comic books), representation is even lower.

Black talent in Hollywood is twice as likely to be **funneled toward films that explicitly thematize race and racism,** which are also among the least-funded.

A 2018 study showed that **78 percent of MENA characters** on television are portrayed as trained terrorists/agents, soldiers, or tyrants.

Of all the top-billed Latino/a characters in the 200 most popular movies, **28 percent** were portrayed as criminals; **17 percent** were poor; **21 percent** were angry.

Between 2007 and 2018, 3 percent of the top-grossing 1,200 films were **directed by Latino/a people. ONE was directed by a woman**.

The top executives of "the big four" publishing houses are white, as are **85 percent of the people who acquire and edit books.**

Scavenger Hunt!

DIRECTIONS:
• Write in an answer for each category. It can be something you already know about or something you look up online!
• When you're done, circle the titles you have *not* read/watched/listened to.
• Voila! You have a list of ideas for how you can diversify your feed! What will you *watch, read,* and *listen* to next?!

A book of poetry published in the last year by a BIPOC poet:

A podcast hosted by a queer BIPOC person or duo:

THREE films featuring Black leads that aren't about a) trauma, b) slavery, or c) the civil rights movement (and *The Help* doesn't count):

A radio station/show featuring music from around the world:

A memoir by a BIPOC woman with a very different life experience from yours:

THREE children's/YA books that feature a BIPOC protagonist:

THREE "classic" twentieth-century novels written by BIPOC authors:

A BIPOC-focused news outlet (online or print):

A TV show that centers the following in a lead role:
• An AAPI woman
• An Indigenous person
• An LGBTQ+ person
• A MENA person (not portrayed as a terrorist)
• A Latino/a person (not portrayed as a criminal/domestic worker)
• A trans person (played by a trans actor)

A movie that passes the Bechdel Test (named for cartoonist Alison Bechdel, it must feature at least two women who talk to each other about something other than a man):

A movie that passes the DuVernay Test (named for director Ava DuVernay, it's a film/show in which "African Americans and other minorities have fully realized lives rather than serve as scenery in white stories"):

A movie that passes another test that you make up!

The _____ Test:

A film made in and about a country you've never been to:

Social media time! Can you expand your feed to include:
• BIPOC disability justice activist
• Indigenous rights org
• Fat liberation activist
• A Trans rights activist
• BIPOC feminist org
• Electoral justice org
• Climate justice activist
• Prison abolitionist
• Reproductive rights activist
• BIPOC-led gun violence org

BONUS: An ensemble cast of people of color who are just existing in the world doing mundane things, like the white people on *Friends* who got to just . . . be friends:

HOW TO DONATE YOUR MONEY

DIRECTIONS: Get a bingo buddy (or two or three!) and decide on the donation amount per square ($5? $20?). See who can get a Giving bingo first! Complete a row vertically, horizontally, or diagonally to "win"! Leveraging your financial privilege is a powerful way to support racial justice efforts nationwide, and in your own community. And you don't have to be rich: Whether it's $5 or $5,000, what matters is your support.

Get creative with your giving. Think local, think small, think BIPOC-led, and think out of the traditional donating giving box!

Think less about doing it to be charitable, and more about doing it to redistribute wealth and empower impacted communities who know what they need to thrive.

We love big national orgs, but we also love smaller grassroots organizations who work on the ground in the communities they serve. They don't often get big corporate donations or have the capacity to run glitzy fundraising campaigns. When there's a natural disaster it's easy to donate to the Red Cross, but it doesn't take much effort to look up the hard-hit region and find a list of community organizations you might give to instead.

GIVING BINGO

DONORS CHOOSE CLASSROOM IN YOUR AREA	PTA OF TITLE 1 SCHOOL NEAREST YOU	MUTUAL AID FUND NEAR YOU	BAIL FUND FOR PROTESTERS	GOFUNDME OF YOUR CHOICE
ORG SUPPORTING VOTING RIGHTS FOR INDIGENOUS COMMUNITIES	RENT RELIEF FUND NEAR YOU	REPARATIONS FUND	THERAPY FUND FOR BLACK JOURNALISTS	INDIGENOUS LAND TAX FUND
ABORTION FUND FOR STATE W/ LIMITED REPRO RIGHTS ACCESS	IMMIGRATION LEGAL DEFENSE FUND	★	POLITICAL CAMPAIGN FOR A BIPOC WOMAN RUNNING FOR OFFICE	LOCAL FOOD BANK
SCHOLARSHIP FUND FOR YOUTH SPORTS ORG	LOCAL SHELTER/ NONPROFIT FOR LGBTQ+ UNHOUSED YOUTH	COMMUNITY-BASED MENTAL HEALTH CRISIS SERVICES	NONPROFIT FOR BLACK AND INDIGENOUS TRANS WOMEN	BIPOC-LED COMMUNITY ORG IN CITY HIT BY NATURAL DISASTER
COLLEGE FUND FOR FIRST-GEN COLLEGE STUDENT	NATURAL DISASTER RELIEF: DONATE TO ORG IN REGION EXPERIENCING NATURAL DISASTER	BREAKING NEWS: DONATE TO ORG IN REGION EXPERIENCING TRAUMA	HELP SOMEONE PAY FOR A SERVICE ANIMAL	HELP SOMEONE FUND THEIR JOY

 **EXTRA TIPS**

1 **Choose an organization and opt to make recurring monthly donations**, rather than giving in one lump sum. Recurring donations are especially helpful for smaller organizations: It helps them spread the financial impact throughout the year, not just during fundraising drives.

2 **Set aside a percentage of your monthly/annual income to donate.** This can include recurring monthly donations, as well as "discretionary" funds that can be used for a GoFundMe or other urgent fundraiser.

3 **Matching donations!** Do you work for a company that offers matching donations? Take advantage of it, and help direct even more funds to small grassroots organizations.

4 Money isn't the only thing you can give: **You can volunteer your time, or provide material items.** Always check before donating used items—organizations don't want bags of junk! Check to see if local shelters and nonprofits have wish lists, and give only what they ask for.

PROTESTER PAPER DOLL

FLIP TO THE BACK OF THE BOOK FOR A PLAYABLE VERSION OF THIS PAPER DOLL!

WKB: What do we want?

KS: Protester paper dolls!

WKB: When do we want them?

KS: Now!

WKB: Great! Here ya go.

KS: This activity is inspired by my daughter, who made an elaborate paperdoll protest after we went to the Women's March in 2017.

WKB: Showing up to protests and marches is a key part of pretty much every movement for social justice.

KS: Protests can be empowering and impactful, celebratory and fun.

WKB: They can also be dangerous. Because police have weapons. And tear gas is no joke.

KS: So even if the event you're showing up to is *probably* going to be mellow and nonviolent, you should always be prepared so that you can be safe.

STAY SAFE
- Go with a buddy and have a safety plan.
- Tell a friend where you'll be.
- Know who organized the protest.
- Check accommodations in advance: Safe for kids? ASL interpreter? ADA accessible? Restrooms?
- Be aware of your surroundings at all times.
- Have an exit strategy to get out of the crowd.
- Know where the cops are.
- Stay calm if things get heated.
- Leave if you feel unsafe.

Comfortable, closed-toed shoes are best.

Keep a "protest pack" stocked with sunscreen, snacks, water, tampons, First Aid kit, phone charger, etc.

YOU HAVE THE RIGHT TO
- Peacefully assemble
- Photograph/film anything in plain view, including the police
- Protest in public spaces
- Distribute leaflets + literature
- Speak out on public property
- March in the streets/on sidewalks, as long as traffic isn't blocked
- Remember: Private property rules are different!

DO THE WORK
- For more details about your rights as a protester and citizen observer, go to the ACLU's website.

- Learn about the National Lawyers Guild, whose observers often attend large protests wearing distinctive bright green hats.

- Learn about bail funds that get set up to help free arrested protesters.

DON'T WEAR
- ✕ Valuable jewelry or watches
- ✕ Flip-flops, heels, or any shoes you can't run in
- ✕ Contact lenses—chemicals can get trapped behind them (if you have to wear contacts, bring protective goggles)

Bandanas soaked in milk/vinegar help you breathe through chemicals.

COLORING BREAK!

It's Levar Burton! He's been doing the work for years, leveraging his platform to promote literacy and the power of storytelling. Color him in (maybe while watching an old episode of *Reading Rainbow?*)!

CHAPTER

5

Keep On Keepin' On

Guess what? You're ready to always be doing the work! Yep, you can make antiracist work an integrated, sustainable part of your life. In this chapter you'll learn how to do things like:

⇨ Put your activism on the calendar.

⇨ Make mistakes, and make amends.

⇨ Evolve your language.

⇨ Build your capacity to creatively imagine a future free of white supremacy.

SUPPLIES

PARTNER   PEN/PENCIL   INTERNET

CALENDAR   ART SUPPLIES

This book comes out of a very specific present moment, and it includes a lot of information about the past.

But this book is really about the FUTURE.

KS: And how we can work to build a better one for generations to come.

WKB: And what tools you're going to need to make that happen.

KS: Remember the beginning of this book where we talked about Jane Elliott and the exercise she did with her audiences? How once you acknowledge that you know what's happening, you can't NOT do anything about it?

WKB: Indeed.

KS: That's it. That's the tweet. You know what is happening. In part, because we've been telling you in excruciating detail throughout this book.

WKB: Hopefully it hasn't been too excruciating. There were a couple good jokes.

KS: So now you just know. And you know you know. And you can't unknow it.

WKB: Yay! You're done! YOU DID THE—

KS: ['80s cartoon villain voice] Not so fast!

WKB: Womp womp! Maybe there are a few more things we should talk about.

KS: Like how to actually keep doing the work, once you finish this book. And what to do if you fuck up and get it wrong.

WKB: You mean WHEN you fuck up and get it wrong!

KS: Exactly. None of this is easy. Sorry! It's just not.

WKB: The epic journey of eradicating racist bullshit from this land is long and arduous. As you strive to reach the promised land of equity and justice, you will undoubtedly encounter some obstacles. And if you get bogged down or feel like you can't move on, do what I do. Think of Harriet Tubman staring at you and saying, "Oh. . . . Is this too hard for you? Is it more difficult than you imagined?"

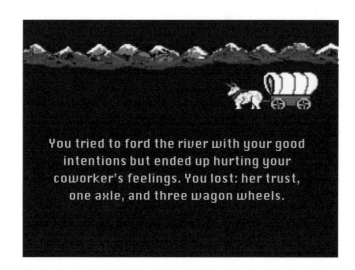

You tried to ford the river with your good intentions but ended up hurting your coworker's feelings. You lost: her trust, one axle, and three wagon wheels.

When it comes to doing the work, what are you worried about? Check all that apply:

○ Not knowing where to start

○ Losing momentum

○ Burning out

○ Getting sleepy

○ Feeling overwhelmed

○ Fucking up

○ Staying positive

○ Saying or doing the wrong thing

○ Losing friends and family

○ Not doing enough

○ Not being able to integrate racial justice work into my life in meaningful ways.

○ Forgetting to do the work when I promised to do the work

○ Having patience

○ Being an introvert who's not used to speaking up

○ Feeling confused about what to do and when

○ Feeling snacky

○ SQUIRREL!

WKB: These are all really common concerns that folks have.

KS: Here's what we want you to do: Read the ones you checked off out loud.

WKB: For real, say them out loud: "I'm worried about not knowing where to start."

KS: Now imagine someone you love, respect, and trust saying this. Imagine it's your best friend! What advice would you give them?

WKB: Are you going to say, "Now give yourself that same advice"? And maybe add, "And do it with as much compassion and encouragement as you'd give them!"

KS: Precisely. I often hear white people talk about how the fear of getting it wrong can be debilitating. They're so afraid to screw up that they say nothing.

WKB: That silence is really damn loud.

KS: For white people, part of moving past that is accepting our capacity to cause harm, and acknowledging the inherent violence of our whiteness. It can be a hard pill to swallow, but if we can understand that our white skin comes with harm, like it's part of the base model, we can be better prepared to respond and repair when harm occurs.

WKB: One of the most important things that any person committed to doing the work can learn is that the question is not "What if I fuck up?" but "When I do fuck up, what am I going to do about it?"

KS: You will fuck up!

In fact, you already have. And it's quite possible that nobody told you.

Sit with that for a moment or two. It's about impact not intent, remember?

> "If I can see the ways I am perpetuating systemic oppressions, if I can see where I learned the behavior and how hard it is to unlearn it, I start to have more humility as I see the messiness of the communities I am part of, the world I live in."
>
> —adrienne maree brown, WE WILL NOT CANCEL US

WKB: We would like to offer you a 1,000 percent guarantee that you, armed with all the best, shiniest gold-star woke intentions, will mess up at some point. We say this because it has happened to us—and we'll get to that in a second.

KS: You'll misgender someone. You'll make a comment that you didn't think was harmful—but turns out, it was. You'll write an impassioned post that you really thought hard about and someone will come through and point out that it's problematic. You'll retweet 140 characters from a guy you think is the right person to retweet but is actually a shady scammer who's been routinely discredited by Black women and then you're confused because you thought he was legit but another person you follow says he's not and—

WKB: Are you talking about—

KS: Yup. So anyway: I'm going to go out on a limb here and say that most people reading this book do not want to upset or offend or demean or hurt others, especially when it comes to issues of race and racism. In fact, I'm pretty sure that most of you are actually terrified of this happening. That's a super reasonable anxiety! It means you give a shit!

WKB: It sucks to be wrong. It sucks to hear that your words or actions hurt someone. But it usually sucks more for the person who was harmed. And if that person mustered the energy to come to you with feedback (and let's be honest—most of us don't enjoy confrontation), well . . . that also sucks for them. Especially if they're a person of color who has done this before and has experienced the White Tear Deluge.

KS: So the question isn't "What if I fuck up?" But "When I fuck up, how can I repair the harm and do better next time?" You can't let that fear hold you back from doing what's right and necessary. I hear this so often from white people, that the fear of getting it wrong can be immobilizing. So they say and do nothing. It's real.

BE

Humble
"Oof. I really got that wrong."

Gracious
"I appreciate you taking the time to let me know this."

Curious
"I'm definitely going to learn more."

Transparent
"It's been brought to my attention that the name we came up with for the campaign is ableist. I didn't realize that, and now I do, because Kim spoke up."

Motivated
"I'm really excited to share this feedback with my team. We can make this idea so much better."

DON'T BE

Defensive
"Are you telling me I'm racist?!"

Dismissive
"This is how I've always done it, and no one has ever complained."

Dramatic
[Sobs uncontrollably]

Defeatist
"What's the point of even trying? It seems like everything I do is going to be problematic."

We #@%*!'d up!

@$&*! Live At 10: Local Racism Expert Makes Mistake! By W. Kamau Bell

IT WAS MAY, 2020. Actually, it was June . . . Actually it was May into June. Who can remember? I was getting hit up by EVERYBODY to talk about racism, white supremacy, George Floyd's murder, the coronavirus, Minneapolis, Trump, white privilege, #BlackLivesMatter, and ESPN's *The Last Dance*. (Okay, maybe not so much that one.) Eventually, I would joke that I was every white talk show host's Black friend.

I was also getting a lot of requests to do local news. And while I don't get much of my news from local news, I respect it. When they ask me to come on, I try to do it. I assume I'm there to say some of the things that they are contractually bound not to say. I believe that's how local anchor Kristen Sze got to me. She wanted me to come on to do what I do.

I had done her show years ago, and remembered her being funny and kind. I was happy to return to talk about the national "racial reckoning."

The Zoom began, and Kristen and I had the awkward, stutter-stepping Zoom hello. She let me know she was excited to have me on, and she said that it was nice to meet me.

ME: We've met before . . . I was on your show with the . . . *[can' t think of the name]* . . . the weatherman . . . the Black weatherman . . . Spencer?

KRISTEN: *[Looking slightly awkward]*: Actually, that wasn't me. That was Janelle Wang.

ME: *[Wanting to quickly die, realizing I have just mistaken her for the other Asian newscaster]*: . . .

KRISTEN: It's okay. People mistake us for each other all the time.

ME: Umm . . . I'm . . . so . . . sor . . .

KRISTEN: It's fine. We actually went to school together. We have been friends for years.

ME: *[Sill wanting to die]*: OK . . . umm . . . I'm so . . . sorry.

Then the cameras rolled and we were on live TV.

Even though we weren't live when it happened, I couldn't let it go. I was supposed to be one of America's premiere racism experts (in, like, the college dropout division). And I failed Racism 101 instead. Or—maybe I had just passed Racist 101. This was bad. Real bad. And Kristen was already firing questions off as if I were an expert on how to participate in the racial reckoning.

I got my mental equilibrium back, answering her questions with wit and realness—and then Kristen shifted gears.

KRISTEN: Before we went on the air you called me by the name of another Asian American broadcaster.

She didn't do it in a gotcha way. It was more in a "let's walk it like YOU talk it" way. In that moment I could have been defensive or short with her, but in a way I was grateful.

ME: *[Shakily wading into the deep water]*: I'm glad we got to that. Yes, I mistook you for a different person who works at ABC News who is of course Asian American. *[I felt like I needed to repeat this point so it didn't seem like I was avoiding it.]* And I'm owning it right here because this is how it works.

KRISTEN: *[Giving me more room to operate]*: It is how it works.

ME: *[Holding up my arm to the camera]*: I have goose pimples right now as we talk about it because I know people on Twitter are going to be like "arghhhhhhhhh," and yet this is how it works. Own your mistake. Step into the mistake. Step through the mistake.

And then we moved on.

SUFFRAGETTE CITY By Kate Schatz

IN JANUARY 2016, my friend Leslie and I decided to start an organization intended to engage local women in meaningful, coordinated political activism. I was sick of hearing friends and acquaintances—many of whom were white moms like me—voice dismay in the wake of the most recent horrific event (the latest mass shooting, the latest police murder caught on video) but not following up with action. With the 2016 election just 11 months ahead, we decided it was time to get these women on board, once a month, for a house party that was also a kind of activist training ground. We would hold the parties on Sunday afternoons, and focus on a different issue each month—like gun control, racial justice, reproductive rights, and the climate crisis. We'd phonebank and write letters and call our elected officials. And by the time the election came near these women would be engaged and activated and ready to help elect our first woman president! And we would provide snacks! And wine! And childcare! We would call it . . .

SUFFRAGETTE SUNDAYS!

The perfect name! Catchy and cute, but also strong, with a nod toward history and the women who fought for over 80 years so that we could cast our ballots for Hillary!

For 10 months we held regular meetings in our homes, calling ourselves Suffragette Sundays. About 30–50 people, mostly white women, showed up each month, ready to take action. We wanted to be inclusive and intersectional. We reached out to nonwhite friends. We invited Black women to speak. We took action on racial justice. We started a Facebook group that grew to about 900 members. Word spread, and more people showed up each month. They continued to be mostly white women.

And then came the election. Our ranks suddenly swelled—the Facebook group grew to 10,000 as approximately half of the country lost its collective shit and tried to figure out the 2016 version of "what can I dooooo?" Requests to start chapters in other cities came pouring in. We were flooded with emails, comments, requests. And in the midst of it all, we got some feedback.

"About the name," one Black woman said. "It makes it feel . . . like a white women's group." "It doesn't make me feel welcome," echoed another woman. "Honestly, a lot of those 'suffragettes' were full-on racists. The name is problematic."

So. There it was. My brilliant, clever name choice was actively excluding the very people we wanted to include. I was bummed. Because people felt harmed—but also because I really liked the name. I went into a spiral. We'd been using the name all year! It had traction and recognizability and alliteration. It was in my email signature! We'd made cute iron-on sashes modeled after the ones worn by early twentieth-century suffrage activists who literally risked their lives for the vote! And yes, Susan B. Anthony was racist and eager to deny Black men the right to vote in order to protect superior white womanhood, but there were many Black suffrage activists as well, and I had written posts highlighting their work, and but and but but. . . . If we changed the name that would mean admitting that I was . . . wrong. Another white woman who fucked up. Oh, shit.

The name itself was a barrier to entry. The impact of the name was harmful, a signal that this group of mostly white women hadn't thought some shit through. It didn't matter whether I'd written a post about Ida B. Wells—the name was a red flag for Black women wondering if this would be a safe space for them. And several women had taken the time and energy to come to me with that feedback. THAT was what mattered—not my ego, not my Great Idea.

We changed the name.

It wasn't hard. We listened to the feedback, and we thought of a better name. Solidarity Sundays. It had the same alliteration, and it spoke to what we really needed in the wake of that election. I wrote a post about the name change and shared it with the group. I was direct and honest about the feedback we received, and our decision to change the name.

And people liked it. Solidarity Sundays grew and expanded over the next several years. We engaged thousands of women, including a number of members who ended up running for office. Did we make plenty of other missteps in the process of organizing and maintaining it all? Definitely. But that's another anecdote.

We could have dug in and gotten defensive. We could have spun our wheels and panicked and cried. We could have made excuses. Or, we could just make the change and move it along. I'm glad we did.

NOPE OR NICE?

Understanding the history of the words and phrases we use is part of understanding how racism has shaped American culture. It's also a big part of figuring out how to NOT fuck up. What you say MATTERS. And even if you would never use an overt slur, you might have words in your vocab that are rooted in racist ideas and histories, and that are hurtful to others.

Some of these words and phrases listed here are offensive to one or more groups of people.

Some are totally fine (for now).

If you realize you've been using a word that we think is a NOPE? Ultimately you decide what to say and not say, but FYI: It's pretty easy to switch it up and stop using certain words. Language evolves, and so can we.

The more you know, the better you do.

DIRECTIONS: Read these words and phrases and decide whether each one is a NOPE, or whether it's NICE. CIRCLE the ones that are "nice" and put an X through the ones that are a "nope."

Gypped

All lives matter

Silver lining

Easy peasy lemon squeezy

Off the reservation

Ghetto

Sold down the river

Howdy

A-OK

Scuttlebutt

Uppity

Colored people

Blackmail

Jew down

Powwow

Master bedroom

Spirit animal

Literally any sports team that references Indigenous Americans

Dog leg

Indian-style

Exotic

Jew down
NOPE—This is an antisemitic phrase rooted in sterotypes about Jewish people being stingy with money. Instead say: haggle; negotiate; bargain.

Master bedroom
NOPE—In this context, the word "master" is associated with a person who controls or dominates another. This term, along with "master bathroom," is being phased out in the real estate and architecture worlds, due to its ties to slavery—homes had "slave quarters," as well as areas designated for the "master." Alternate terms include "primary bedroom" and "main bedroom." Or just, like, "bedroom."

Spirit animal
NOPE—The phrase is commonly used in a joking way to describe an animal or object that represents someone's personal qualities ("That pug is totally my spirit animal!"). But for many Indigenous people, the casual, facetious usage (especially by white people) is problematic, because the phrase has spiritual and religious meaning. Can the pug be your kindred spirit? Can you just say "IT ME!"

Dog leg
NICE—Until dogs learn to talk, in which case they might let us know that they'd prefer us to use another term to refer to something that bends sharply or takes a hard turn.

Indian-style
NOPE—When we were kids this was the term for sitting cross-legged, which is actually a fine way to describe sitting with your legs crossed. But if you need another term, how about "criss-cross-applesauce," which, thankfully, has become the preferred phrase for many educators, and doesn't rely on an untrue stereotype about how an entire group of people sit.

All lives matter
HELL NO—Just, nope. Periodt.

Easy peasy lemon squeezy
NICE—good news, you can still say this. Lemons are cool, and not racist.

Ghetto
NOPE—unless you're using it to describe historically Jewish neighborhoods ."Ghetto" is often used as a pejorative to describe someone's less-than-"proper" (aka white) clothes, behavior, or appearance. It's also used as shorthand for low-income neighborhoods, and as code for "Black and brown people live here." So when a city council member says "We don't want downtown turning into a ghetto," we all know what he means. Right?

Howdy
NICE—"Howdy" is a greeting common in the American South and West, and is a shortened form of "How do you do." Can't guarantee that folks throughout history who've said howdy aren't racist themselves, but the term itself is A-OK.

A-OK
NICE—Since we just used it, we thought we'd look it up and check. Fun fact: "A-OK" comes from NASA engineers who used it during early radio transmission tests because the sound of "A" was sharper and easier to hear than the softer sound of "O."

Uppity
NOPE—The word itself means arrogant, self-important, snobby. Fine. But also: not fine, because of the long history of how the word has been used to describe Black folks who dared to rise above their assigned position of subordinance (look up how many Republicans have called the Obamas "uppity"). Sure, "uppity" can be used to describe a snobby person of any race, but historically, it hasn't. In fact, in many parts of the South, it was often part of a two-word phrase: an "uppity n_____." Instead say: arrogant; snobby; stuck-up.

Blackmail
NICE—Don't worry, blackmail the word is fine. Blackmail the act ... that's your business.

Powwow
NOPE—Unless you're an Indigenous person referring to a traditional tribal gathering and celebration, this is not your word to use. Not cool for non-Indigenous people to use it to refer to meetings ("Let's have a powwow this afternoon to figure that out"). Instead, say: brainstorm; have a meeting; gathering.

Literally any sports team that references Indigenous Americans
NOPE—How have you not changed your name yet? CHANGE YOUR NAME. CHANGE YOUR MASCOT. Your stubborn racism is showing. Clean up that mess.

Exotic
NOPE—"Exotic" is a word that white people love to use to describe "the other." From spices to language to women, it denotes something different and "from somewhere else," and is often employed as a "well-meaning" compliment toward a woman of color. ("Your braids look so exotic!" "I just love the shape of your eyes, so exotic!") You might think you're paying her a compliment, but what you're really doing is objectifying her, and what you're actually saying is "You look different. You're not like me." We'd suggest an alternate phrase, but really—do you need to comment on her appearance at all?!

DO THE READING

- *We Will Not Cancel Us* by adrienne maree brown

- *Why Won't You Apologize* by Dr. Harriet Lerner

- *Fumbling Towards Repair* by Mariame Kaba and Shira Hassan

- *Conflict Is Not Abuse* by Sarah Schulman

Whether you're called out or called in, at some point you're gonna need to know how to apologize. This is a pretty crucial life skill that is quite challenging for a lot of us.

KS: When I think of apology-challenged people, I think of the Great Nipplegate of 2004, when sweet baby Justin Timberlake exposed Janet Jackson's breast to millions of Superbowl viewers, and then offered this wack-ass shit:

"I am sorry that anyone was offended by the wardrobe malfunction during the halftime performance of the Super Bowl. It was not intentional and is regrettable." —Justin Timberlake

HERE ARE SOME TIPS FOR GOOD APOLOGIES

FOCUS ON THE IMPACT, NOT THE INTENT

👍 "That was absolutely inappropriate of me. I'm sorry that I did that."

👎 *"I'm sorry if you feel hurt, that was not my intention."*

OWN UP TO WHAT HAPPENED

👍 "Hello everyone, I'm writing with an apology. Yesterday I used an acronym that I thought was clever. A team member privately let me know that it's a racial slur in some parts of the world. I had no idea, but now I do. I'm sorry for any harm this caused, and am grateful to our colleague for stepping up and letting me know.

👎 Whoopsie!

FOCUS ON YOUR ACTIONS, NOT HOW THE INJURED PARTY RESPONDED

👍 "I'm sorry I chose to wear a culturally offensive costume."

👎 *"I'm sorry you were offended by my costume, but I did not deserve to be called racist for it! You need to lighten up."*

INCLUDE A CLEAR AND APPROPRIATE FOLLOW-UP WITHOUT GOING OVER THE TOP

👍 "I'm taking that word out of my vocabulary, and I'm going to share posts from Indigenous activists so my followers can understand it, too."

👎 *"I will never ever say that word again in my entire life, and if I ever hear anyone say it I will never forgive them, and I'm going to do everything I can to seek justice for Indigenous people everywhere!"*

DON'T INCLUDE THE WORD "BUT"

👍 "I'm so sorry for what I did."

👎 *"I'm so sorry for what I did. But—"*

DON'T CENTER ON YOUR OWN GUILT/REMORSE

👍 "I take full responsibility for my actions. I'm committed to treating you with the dignity you deserve."

👎 *"I feel so horrible about what happened. I'm honestly losing sleep over this, I just feel like absolute shit, I'm just the worst!"*

DON'T SHIFT BLAME OR MAKE EXCUSES

👍 "It doesn't matter that I was drunk. I should not have done that. Period."

👎 *"I'm so sorry! I was wasted!"*

DON'T REQUIRE FORGIVENESS

👍 "I know these are just words. Hopefully my actions from here on out will show I'm committed to doing better. Until then, no need to reply."

👎 *"I just hope you can forgive me. Please, you know I'm not a bad person, I'm not racist!"*

DO THE WORK

Now that you've seen all these examples, rewrite Justin Timberlake's apology (then look up the apology he issued to Britney Spears and Janet Jackson in 2021).

Go back to your example of the time you messed up. If you could do it over, how would you apologize? Write it all out in the box on the following page.

Want to learn more about effective apologies and repairing harm? Check out:
• *Why Won't You Apologize?* by Dr. Harriet Lerner
• *Conflict Is Not Abuse* by Sarah Schulman

DO THE WORK

DIRECTIONS: Reflect on a time when you got it wrong, then answer the questions below.

What happened?

Did you apologize? If yes, how? If not, why?

Knowing what you know now, what could you have done differently?

Get an Accountability Partner

WKB: Accountability is about keeping your commitments. Doing that thing you said you were gonna do—and ideally, doing it well.

KS: Easier said than done.

WKB: Remember the summer of 2020 when everyone was suddenly very enlightened and aware and all the corporations were like WE LOVE BLACK PEOPLE!!! and they made grand public statements and promised to do better and . . . then . . . didn't actually do better?

KS: It's easy to say you're going to do something—it's much harder to do it. This is accountability.

WKB: Find one person in your life who is willing to do this work with you. It's the buddy system, but for dismantling white supremacy.

KS: For white people, having an accountability partner who's also white is an excellent idea. It can keep you from going to BIPOC folks with questions and emotions that they don't need to hear, and can create a safe space to explore the gnarled nuances of whiteness.

WKB: For BIPOC folks, an accountability partner can help you examine the ways racism and anti-Blackness color the way you move through the world, and strategize what to do about it.

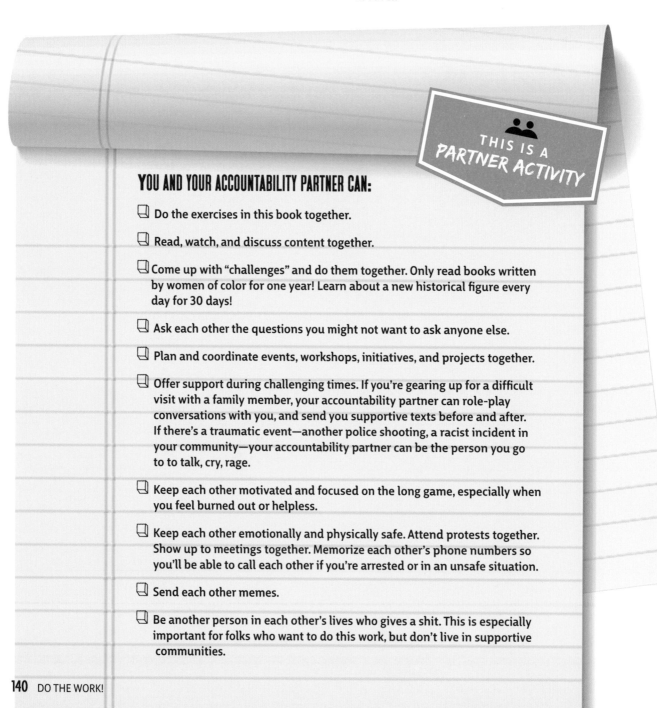

THIS IS A PARTNER ACTIVITY

YOU AND YOUR ACCOUNTABILITY PARTNER CAN:

☐ Do the exercises in this book together.

☐ Read, watch, and discuss content together.

☐ Come up with "challenges" and do them together. Only read books written by women of color for one year! Learn about a new historical figure every day for 30 days!

☐ Ask each other the questions you might not want to ask anyone else.

☐ Plan and coordinate events, workshops, initiatives, and projects together.

☐ Offer support during challenging times. If you're gearing up for a difficult visit with a family member, your accountability partner can role-play conversations with you, and send you supportive texts before and after. If there's a traumatic event—another police shooting, a racist incident in your community—your accountability partner can be the person you go to to talk, cry, rage.

☐ Keep each other motivated and focused on the long game, especially when you feel burned out or helpless.

☐ Keep each other emotionally and physically safe. Attend protests together. Show up to meetings together. Memorize each other's phone numbers so you'll be able to call each other if you're arrested or in an unsafe situation.

☐ Send each other memes.

☐ Be another person in each other's lives who gives a shit. This is especially important for folks who want to do this work, but don't live in supportive communities.

ACCOUNTABILITY PARTNER CONTRACT

On this date_____, in the fine city of _____,
W. Kamau Bell and Kate Schatz hereby proclaim _____
and _____ to be ACCOUNTABILITY PARTNERS in doing
the damn work.

_____ and _____ promise to support each
other for as long as possible in their sincere and undaunted efforts
to be less racist and to root out and eradicate white supremacy in
all spaces it resides (which is basically most spaces). They will do
this by:

And also _____.

And probably _____.

And maybe even _____.

Signed:

_____

_____

Date: _____

SCHEDULE THE WORK!

We hear you saying "I want to get involved but I'm just so busy!"

Not many of us have endless hours to devote to changing the world. And real talk: Community organizing and racial justice advocacy does not come with a desirable salary. There are many incredible people serving their communities in powerful ways, and we are beyond grateful for them. If it's not your full-time world, but you want to make advocating for racial justice a regular part of your life, consider doing what you already do to keep track of all the activities, obligations, and upcoming events: PUT IT ON THE CALENDAR.

COMMIT!

You can't do everything all the time, but you can do specific things at specific times. Change happens because multitudes of people commit to working over long periods of time. It's incremental—what you do today, tomorrow, and next week matters. Here are some ideas for how you can make doing the work a recurring event.

☐ Schedule "action hours" (or half-hours) into your weeks, and use this time to do whatever feels urgent—calling elected officials about a pending bill, drafting your statement for the city council meeting, posting to social media about an issue you're working on.

☐ READ A BOOK! Set aside a time each week to put down the phone and pick up a book from the Do the Reading list in the back of this book!

☐ CATCH UP ON THE NEWS. Set aside time to read the paper, watch the news, and/or listen to podcasts that keep you informed on current events.

☐ Have a monthly Family Movie Night, where you watch a family-friendly movie with a BIPOC lead, diverse cast, and positive message.

☐ Choose an issue or cause to commit to—for a week, a month, a year—and set aside time for research and learning, as well as planning and doing.

☐ Mark cultural holidays on your calendar. What special days are coming up each month? Learn about ones you're not familiar with, both for your own enrichment and for the benefit of your community. Know when Lunar New Year begins! Don't schedule meetings on Yom Kippur! Understand why some of your students may have low energy during Ramadan!

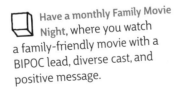

☐ Choose a monthly Donation Day! Need ideas for where to put your money? Check the Donation Bingo activity for suggestions.

☐ Create your own special "holidays"—we all know they gave Black history February because it's the shortest damn month. If April 3 can be National Chocolate Mousse Day and October 2 can be National Name Your Car Day, anything is possible. National Reparations Day? National End White Supremacy Day? National Talk to Your Racist Family Members Week?!

☐ Celebrate Activist Birthdays. Pick someone who inspires you, put their birthday on your calendar, and come up with ways to celebrate them.

☐ Reminder to breathe! Set a reminder for the middle of each weekday to pause, breathe, and remind yourself that you care. Get up and stretch and take a walk.

☐ Take time to reflect. Maybe take five minutes on Fridays after work to look back at the week and reflect on your actions, or ten minutes on Sunday night to consider the work for the week ahead.

DO THE WORK MONTHLY PLANNER

Choose an upcoming month, and fill in the dates. What holidays and events might you honor? What activists and historical figures were born in this month? What time can you set aside for doing some work?

MONTH _____

YEAR _____

TO-DO LIST

FLIP TO THE BACK OF THE BOOK FOR POP-OUT CARDS YOU CAN STICK ON YOUR FRIDGE.

I'M GOING TO

☐ **READ**

_____

☐ **WATCH**

_____

☐ **LISTEN TO**

_____

☐ **DONATE TO**

_____

☐ **LEARN ABOUT**

_____

☐ **GIVE A SHIT ABOUT**

_____

REMINDERS

☞ **BRUSH + FLOSS MY TEETH**

☞ **WASH MY HANDS (WITH SOAP!)**

☞ **GET ENOUGH SLEEP**

☞ **STOP ACTING LIKE RACISM ISN'T MY PROBLEM, TOO**

☞ _____

☞ _____

☞ _____

☞ _____

☞ _____

BIG LIST of ACTIONS
YOU CAN TAKE

Not sure what you can do to make a difference? We compiled a list!
These ideas come from people who live all over the country,
in all kinds of different communities.
Tear it out, and get to work.

⇨ Join the diversity and inclusion group at your work. If there isn't one, get it started.

⇨ **Are you involved in hiring? Recruit from historically Black colleges and universities.**

⇨ Do you sit on a corporate, nonprofit, or arts board? Don't confirm any additional white board members.

⇨ **Refuse to be on all-white or all-male panels.**

⇨ Planning a protest or public action? Make sure it's designed with disabled people in mind.

⇨ **Offer to run errands for neighbors who might appreciate the support, including single parents and the elderly.**

⇨ Advocate for pay equity within your field or company. Make sure interns get paid!

⇨ **Give away what you don't use! Sites like Freecycle help reduce waste and encourage reuse and sharing.**

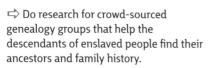

⇨ **Fight voter suppression with grassroots organizations in your state or national groups such as Fair Fight Action or Black Voters Matter.**

⇨ Campaign and raise money for the progressive candidates you believe can make change in your city, county, and state.

⇨ **If something you care about isn't getting the attention it deserves, write a proposed policy, form a coalition around it, and take it to your city council, school board, or state capitol.**

⇨ Pay attention to global events.

⇨ If you use social media, follow people from other countries who are doing work that aligns with your interests.

⇨ Start with the desired outcome and work backward to find your role in making it real.

⇨ **Choose a few respected newspapers from major cities in other countries and read them regularly.**

⇨ VOTE!

⇨ **Run for office! From the school board to the Senate, consider a campaign.**

⇨ Check in regularly with Black and brown leaders in trans, disability justice, climate justice, and fat liberation communities. Support their needs!

⇨ Do research for crowd-sourced genealogy groups that help the descendants of enslaved people find their ancestors and family history.

⇨ **Write your representatives and tell them to end qualified immunity of police.**

⇨ Outraged by a news story? Use the internet to find on-the-ground organizations already working on it. Do and share what they say.

Who's going to help you do this work?
List THREE people you want to share ideas with.

COMMUNITY

⇨ Greet community members in the languages they speak.

⇨ Start a Little Free Library and stock it with antiracist literature and books by BIPOC authors. Bonus if you make it a food pantry, too!

⇨ Facilitate ways for people in prison to gain literacy. Illiteracy rates in prisons are 75 percent, and it's near-impossible to navigate the post-prison world without reading and writing skills.

⇨ Volunteer with a local organization that supports unhoused people.

⇨ Attend local city council meetings. Who else is showing up? Whose voices are the loudest? Who's already doing the work you want to be doing?

⇨ Attend and fund local community celebrations and commemorations such as Lunar New Year, Juneteenth, Day of Remembrance, and Día de los Muertos.

⇨ Ask Black-led organizations how you can help and then do what they say!

⇨ Join your local chapter of SURJ (Showing Up for Racial Justice).

⇨ Use your special skills! Cook for an event. Host a fundraiser. Offer legal or tech support services to activist organizations. Donate pro bono care work, therapy, or legal advice to BIPOC-led orgs.

⇨ Give reparations. Put aside $20–$100 a month and contribute to a GoFundMe, DonorsChoose, or other fundraiser started by Black folks.

⇨ Start a giving circle.

⇨ Volunteer for the campaigns for local officials and ballot initiatives that you support.

⇨ Review the diversity statement of any organizations in which you participate. Does the org's reality reflect the values it expressed in the statement? Is it actively antiracist?

⇨ Are you part of a church or faith community that's doing racial justice work? If they're not, get it started!.

⇨ Don't let people talk shit about Black- or Brown-majority schools in your presence.

⇨ Find BIPOC health care providers for yourself and your family.

⇨ Push for prioritizing investment— from housing down to food purchasing— in BIPOC communities, with the understanding that it has always been prioritized for white men.

⇨ Make sure your book club reads books by BIPOC writers.

⇨ Talk to your neighbors, both housed and unhoused.

⇨ Do you know about mutual aid? Are there any mutual aid projects in your community? If so, support them. If not, consider starting one.

⇨ If you're white, learn how to organize other white people to take action without being righteous know-it-alls.

⇨ Send your kids to public school and help your local schools get the resources they need.

⇨ Keep extra cash and supplies (bottled water, hotel soaps and shampoos, clean socks, packaged snacks) in your car to share with unhoused community members in need.

⇨ Find opportunities for your children to play and learn with a diverse group of children. Bias starts at an early age, but so do acceptance and love.

⇨ Offer to provide childcare for a parent so they can show up and do the work.

⇨ Talk with and listen to people who don't agree with you. Host a community "skill share" event and take turns teaching each other useful skills.

⇨ Extra fruits and veggies from your garden? Share with your neighbors.

FREE

CIRCLE the things you want to do!

⇨ **Like coffee? Buy from a Black-owned roaster. Like weed? Buy from a BIPOC-owned dispensary. Candles, cookies, cleaning supplies, cauliflower, and cosmetics can come from new places.**

⇨ Buy antiracist/multicultural books for the children in your life regardless of their ethnic/racial backgrounds. Buy extra copies and donate them to local libraries, schools, pediatric facilities, etc.

⇨ **Buy a subscription to your local newspaper and READ IT. Know what's going on in your town.**

⇨ Become a monthly subscriber to a Black wine club, CSA, Patreon, OnlyFans, coffee roaster, publication . . .

⇨ **Pay digital creators for the content you appreciate.**

⇨ Make a list of companies that use prison labor and avoid buying from them.

⇨ **Make new friends who are different from you.**

⇨ Ask how others would like/prefer to be introduced.

⇨ **Put your pronouns in your email signature, Zoom screen, name tag, social media bio.**

⇨ Find a financial advisor who can help you transition into racial justice investing.

⇨ Sit with children and elders and listen to them. Offer them your attention, respect, and curiosity.

⇨ **Don't dress your kids in racist or stereotypical Halloween costumes.**

⇨ Shut down racist talk whenever and wherever you hear it.

⇨ **Be intentional about your words and actions.**

⇨ Put a sign in your yard or window.

⇨ **Interrogate your relationship with your white partner. Hold them accountable.**

⇨ Learn how to apologize.

⇨ **Give the land you own back to Indigenous people.**

⇨ Share/repost positive content by and about BIPOC, particularly Black men.

⇨ **Get curious about what makes you uncomfortable. Do ideas like prison abolition, reparations, or universal healthcare seem radical, impractical, or beyond your comfort zone? If so, why?**

⇨ Discover your own hidden biases by taking an Implicit Association Test like the one offered online by Project Implicit.

⇨ Be brave because even quiet voices can be impactful when they speak.

⇨ **Sign up for a training to develop a new skill: transformative justice, nonviolent communiation, DEI training, antiracist training, violence interrupting, etc.**

⇨ Disabled BIPOC folks experience specific physical, digital, and social barriers. Learn about these barriers and work to dismantle them.

⇨ **Be willing to give up advantages you didn't earn.**

⇨ Disentangle your pride and your feelings of entitlement. You worked hard, but you also had privileges that others did not. Both of those things can coexist, and that doesn't diminish your accomplishments.

⇨ **Ask why until you get to the core issue.**

⇨ Remember that we are all just humans, and do your best.

⇨ **Pay your domestic workers and caretakers a living wage.**

⇨ Check out Hand in Hand (domesticemployers.org) to learn how to ethically employ someone in your home.

What ideas can YOU add?

PATIENT NAME
ADDRESS

"...try to spend time with ...uch older activists who ...mind me how much has ...ctually changed."

PATIENT NAME
ADDRESS

"I create intention around who and what I surround myself with. Especially when it comes to family or coworkers that do not want to do the work in dismantling white supremacy."

PATIENT NAME
ADDRESS

"I LOOK TO MY CHILDREN AND IMAGINE THE FUTURE I WANT FOR THEM."

PATIENT NAME
ADDRESS

"When I'm burned out and overwhelmed, I've learned to set boundaries. By cutting back, I can focus on the work and the causes that mean most to me."

PATIENT NAME
ADDRESS

"I go into nature as MUCH as possible. It seems to be the only ...necdote that can ...ffuse the noise ...d pain of the ...rld and remind ...e there's a greater ...uch more beautiful) ...e at work."

PATIENT NAME
ADDRESS

"Eat some snacks. Go outside. Cry. Journal."

PATIENT NAME
ADDRESS

"When I am feeling tender and overwhelmed, I do anything that helps me remember that I am a small piece of a very large, generational shift that is taking place and I don't have to be perfect or have "impact" in the way it is defined at social entrepreneurship conferences or on grant applications."

PATIENT NAME
ADDRESS

"Don't read the comments."

RX FOR RESILIENCE

In the end, the best way to do the work is in community. That's why we wrote this book together, and it's why we tapped so many of the folks we respect, admire, and learn from to contribute to it.

We asked them:
How do you keep doing the work?
How do you cultivate resilience?
How do you keep *going*?

Here's some of what these wise friends prescribe.

PATIENT NAME
ADDRESS

"Pick your battles, and choose to put your energy into the efforts that mean the most to you."

PATIENT NAME
ADDRESS

"Always remember to ...ign yourself with the ...ople for whom giving up ...ope (or courage) is not ... option."

PATIENT NAME
ADDRESS

"know what you're FOR. So often we define our activism in terms of what we're against: racism, war, corporate greed. Which is all true and critical. But make sure to ground the work in what you're FOR. What's your vision for the world? How does your work help build the worlds you want—not just resist the ones you're against?"

PATIENT NAME
ADDRESS

"Remember you don't have to attend ALL the events/ rallies/protests, especially if you're not feeling safe, but also just take a break."

PATIENT NAME
ADDRESS

"I remind myself that deciding whether or not to engage with struggle is a privilege."

PATIENT NAME
ADDRESS

"I read about historical ...igures, especially women, who persevered ...n conditions I can't ...ven imagine. That perspective keeps me humble."

PATIENT NAME
ADDRESS

"De-personalizing is huge for me. My actions matter, but I don't matter that much."

PATIENT NAME
ADDRESS

"I hang out with younger activists who remind me of all I don't know and how awesome that is."

PATIENT NAME
ADDRESS

"When it comes to social media, remember you don't need to post about everything that happens, or respond to every outrage-of-the-day."

PATIENT NAME
ADDRESS

"f I feel I've dropped the ...all, I remind myself I ...n always try again."

PATIENT NAME
ADDRESS

"KEEP A JOURNAL OF YOUR WORK, SO YOU CAN LOOK BACK AT IT AND SEE THAT IT DID HELP."

COLORING BREAK

Grace Lee Boggs spent much of her life building resilient communities in Detroit, but she was always attuned to global struggles for freedom. She shared this wisdom in a 2009 interview with *Democracy Now*!

BLACK TO THE FUTURE By Adesina O. Koiki

The theme of this puzzle is "Afrofuturism," a cultural aesthetic and philosophy that connects the histories of the African diaspora to dynamic visions for radical futures.

ACROSS

1 Exam for an aspiring atty.
5 Is ___ (probably will)
12 Union pledge?
13 Resort hotel chain
14 Judo technique
15 Holier-than-thou
16 Janelle Monae's Afrofuturist alter ego
19 Start of many California cities
21 Non-native, to a Hawaiian
22 "Working in a Coal Mine" singer Dorsey
23 Set eyes on
25 Barcelona locale
27 Octavia E. Butler's Afrofuturist literary trilogy
31 When a park may close
34 Nintendo release of 2006
35 Letters on a baseball line score
36 Laugh or cringe, say
37 Labor Day mo.
38 Afrofuturism, for this puzzle
40 Ctrl-___-Del
41 Enjoyed a meal
42 Removed unwanted plants
43 Ryan Coogler's Afrofuturist superhero movie
47 Earlier (to)
48 Kvetchers' exclamations
49 Tiny, to Scots
52 Drive
54 Bit of advice
56 Arena staffer
58 Sun Ra's Afrofuturist sci-fi film
61 Immediate family members
62 Gift for a new dad, often
63 Largest dolphin family member
64 Jerry Rice scored 208 of them: Abbr.
65 Sailor's speed units
66 Split veggies?

DOWN

1 Not express
2 "Have a Coke and a ___" (bygone ad slogan)
3 Title role for Quvenzhané Wallis in 2014
4 Laundry detergent brand
5 Quick stop at the convience store
6 Onset of a master plan, perhaps
7 "___ Little Tenderness" (Otis Redding classic)
8 South African urban settlement created by apartheid legislation
9 In the red
10 Award winner's humble remark
11 One-on-one showdown
12 Fairy tale monster
15 Part of a flight
17 Stubbornly demand
18 Monomaniacal literary captain
24 New mascot for Edmonton's Canadian Football League team
26 Trident-shaped Greek letter
27 Jean-___ Picard (U.S.S. Enterprise captain)
28 Many a middle schooler
29 Worrier's words
30 Exploit
31 ___ Spring (anti-goverment protests of the early 2010s)
32 Poker table giveaway
33 Smartphone arrangements
37 Gets going
38 Prepares to swing
39 Stage name of Grammy winner Gabriella Wilson
41 Part of a mil. address
42 "The reason being?"
44 Holey footwear
45 Flying toy
46 Original Monopoly token
49 Social media button
50 Pilgrim's destination
51 Floor plan calculations
52 [Hey you!]
53 Bygone Apple device with a click wheel
55 "Let ___" (Frozen song)
57 Unappetizing food
59 Repulsed reaction
60 Triage places: Abbr.

Answers on page 156

WKB: That's it, folks!

KS: Really? Just like that? We're . . . done?

WKB: Remember how our editor said the book can't be 10,000 pages long? That we couldn't just keep writing until racism was over?

KS: I do. Ok. It's just . . . I . . .

WKB: What's wrong?

KS: I really *liked* being in this book with you! Having these conversations, sharing these stories, and putting together all these quizzes and activities. And geeking out on *all* the historical research!

WKB: That's really your jam.

KS: What about you? How do you feel about it being over?

WKB: Just like I always do with this work: We did a lot, and racism and white supremacy aren't over yet. And that *sucks*.

KS: Remember those tips about resilience? And the ideas for how to keep going?

WKB: It's not just about what you're *against*. This is also about what you're *for*! This is about what you believe and what you *now know* that you didn't know before. It's about getting strong enough to let other people know these things, even when it is difficult.

KS: Hopefully the work you've done in this book will be something you can look back on as you continue doing the work in the real world.

So while this is the end of this book, it is obviously far from the end of this fight.

WKB: As my oldest daughter says, "It's not goodbye. It's just see you later." So . . .

KS & WKB: SEE YOU LATER, RACISM!

THE OFFICIAL CERTIFICATE OF HAVING
DONE THE WORK!

I, _____ aka _____ officially declare that I have done _____
[YOUR NAME]   [EMBARRASSING PET NAME THAT YOUR PARENTS CALL YOU]   [NUMBER]

percent of this book entitled *Do The Work!* heretofore referred to as _____ .
[WAY YOU WOULD DESCRIBE THIS BOOK TO YOUR RACIST UNCLE]

I absolutely did my _____ . I have learned many
[WRITE IN ONE: BEST, BEST UNDER THE CIRCUMSTANCES, MEDIUM-EST, WORST BUT I REFUSE TO BE TOO HARD ON MYSELF]

things that I didn't know before, but I will never be able to forget _____ . And I can't
[SOMETHING THAT BLEW YOUR MIND]

ever get over my anger about _____ . Also, I laughed really hard at _____ .
[THING IN THE BOOK THAT MAKES YOU ANGRY]   [FUNNY THING]

I definitely feel more prepared to confront racism, especially in _____ .
[SPECIFIC AREA OR SUBJECT THAT YOU FEEL BETTER ABOUT CONFRONTING]

I have to admit that while I appreciate this book, it obviously isn't perfect. I do have some questions

about why they _____ .
[THING THAT YOU THINK WE COULD HAVE DONE BETTER]

And even though I am at the end of the book, I still plan on using _____
[SECTION YOU WANT TO GO BACK TO]

so I can eventually _____ .
[INSERT A GOAL]

And I also have to admit that even though I love both of them, my absolute favorite is _____ .*
[WRITE IN ONE: KATE / KAMAU]

Sorry, _____ .
[NAME OF THE ONE YOU DIDN'T WRITE IN]

While I know I will always be engaged in doing the work to create an antiracist society I will also

work to create a society that is anti _____ , _____ , _____ .
[INSERT THREE OTHER SYSTEMIC PREJUDICES]

So, yay me! I did a _____ part of the work!
[WORD THAT MEANS TINY]

I am now going to reward myself with _____ .
[YOUR FAVORITE TREAT OR FUN ACTIVITY]

AND THEN IT'S BACK TO DOING THE WORK!

*If you didn't pick Kamau, you're racist and this book didn't work.

DIRECTIONS: Envision the future you want. What words and images can you plant in the soil today so that we can harvest a peaceful and just world tomorrow? Draw and write your ideas below!

FREEDOM

Do the Reading

These books about race, racism, white supremacy, American history, and the rich and radiant lives of people of color are pictured in the illustrations on pages 5 and 71 and mentioned throughout the book. What's going in your To Be Read stack?!

☐ *An African American and Latinx History of the United States,* by Paul Ortiz

☐ *All the Women Are White, All the Blacks Are Men, But Some of Us Are Brave,* edited by Akasha (Gloria T.) Hull, Patricia Bell Scott, and Barbara Smith

☐ *American Slavery, American Freedom,* by Edmund S. Morgan

☐ *The Apocalypse of Settler Colonialism,* by Gerald Horne

☐ *Barracoon,* by Zora Neale Hurston

☐ *Beyond Respectability,* by Brittney C. Cooper

☐ *Black Against Empire,* by Joshua Bloom and Waldo E. Martin Jr.

☐ *Black is a Country,* by Nikhil Pal Singh

☐ *Black Reconstruction in America 1860–1880,* by W. E. B. Du Bois

☐ *Black Skin, White Masks,* by Frantz Fanon

☐ *A Black Women's History of the United States,* by Daina Ramey Berry and Kali Nicole Gross

☐ *Citizen,* by Claudia Rankine

☐ *Critical Race Theory: The Key Writings That Formed the Movement,* edited by Kimberlé Crenshaw, Neil Gotanda, Gary Peller, and Kendall Thomas

☐ *The Derrick Bell Reader,* by Richard Delgado

☐ *A Disability History of the United States,* by Kim E. Nielsen

☐ *Eloquent Rage,* by Brittney C. Cooper

☐ *Emergent Strategy,* by adrienne maree brown

☐ *Faces at the Bottom of the Well,* by Derrick Bell

☐ *For Colored Girls Who Have Considered Suicide When the Rainbow Is Enuf,* by Ntozake Shange

☐ *Four Hundred Souls,* edited by Ibram X. Kendi and Keisha N. Blain

☐ *Freedom is a Constant Struggle,* by Angela Y. Davis

☐ *Fumbling Towards Repair,* by Mariame Kaba and Shira Hassan

☐ *Hard Times,* by Studs Terkel

☐ *The History of White People,* by Dr. Nell Irvin Painter

☐ *Hood Feminism,* by Mikki Kendall

☐ *How To Be an Antiracist,* by Ibram X. Kendi

☐ *How To Be Less Stupid About Race,* by Crystal M. Fleming

☐ *How We Get Free: Black Feminism and the Combahee River Collective,* edited by Keeanga-Yamahtta Taylor

☐ *How We Show Up: Reclaiming Family, Friendship, and Community,* by Mia Birdsong

☐ *An Indigenous Peoples' History of the United States,* by Roxane Dunbar-Ortiz

☐ *Iron Cages,* by Ronald Takaki

☐ *Lies My Teacher Told Me,* by James W. Loewen

☐ *Local People,* by John Dittmer

☐ *Making Gay History,* by Eric Marcus

☐ *The March Trilogy,* by Rep. John Lewis, Andrew Aydin, and Nate Powell

☐ *Margins and Mainstreams: Asians in American History and Culture,* by Gary Y. Okihiro

☐ *Me and White Supremacy,* by Layla F. Saad

☐ *Memoir of a Race Traitor,* by Mab Segrest

☐ *The Morning Breaks: The Trial of Angela Davis,* by Bettina Aptheker

☐ *The New Jim Crow* by Michelle Alexander

☐ *Parable of the Sower,* by Octavia E. Butler

☐ *A People's History of the United States,* by Howard Zinn

☐ *Pleasure Activism,* by adrienne maree brown

☐ *The Purpose of Power,* by Alicia Garza

☐ *Racecraft,* by Barbara J. Fields and Karen E. Fields

☐ *Rat F**ked and Unrigged,* by Dave Daley

☐ *Reconstruction,* by Eric Foner

☐ *Sister Outsider,* by Audre Lorde

☐ *Southern Horrors,* by Ida B. Wells

☐ *Stamped,* by Ibram X. Kendi and Jason Reynolds

☐ *The Sum of Us,* by Heather McGhee

☐ *Thick,* by Tressie McMillan Cottom

☐ *Ties That Bind,* by Tiya Miles

☐ *12 Million Black Voices,* by Richard Wright

☐ *A Voice From the South,* by Anna J. Cooper

☐ *The Warmth of Other Suns,* by Isabel Wilkerson

☐ *Wayward Lives, Beautiful Experiments,* by Sadiya Hartman

☐ *We Will Not Cancel Us,* by adrienne maree brown

☐ *When Chickenheads Come Home to Roost,* by Joan Morgan

☐ *Why Won't You Apologize,* by Dr. Harriet Lerner

☐ *Women, Race & Class,* by Angela Y. Davis

☐ *Zami: A New Spelling of my Name,* by Audre Lorde

Activity Answers

WORD SEARCH (page 32)

```
Q U Q Y R X Z O C M N J A M I S S J I Z
I Z Z E C D T E E E L E N N D S Y Z K P
H N W I D A H I C K H N T U M E S R C K
P O S S L I M I W H T E I A J N T D V R
P R L T S T D E Q F R A B L Z E E K Z R
B O I T I U C N R P O N L L K T M Z J U
A I O V J T E A E P V H A Y Y I I H B E
W R A E I B U R P J U S C Z U H C I O L
Y R R S Z L S T A M J S K H D W T U I A
H P R A R O E L I D I H N N I D J E Y M
E Z L B N A V G A O L X E H B I P O C U
L V X A H W M M E H N R S V P T K O O A
M J L R T R S Y Z Y O A S V L O U B A R
E C I L P M O C C A C M L T N E T N I T
D E F E N S I V E F M J E X E F Z Q Z E
H Q K T F F Z M A B W W Y A U V F C E C
G N N H F J B S V B R Y G O X G O J O K
B C C Y D B U H H L P K I E V S B S M Y
D I S C R I M I N A T I O N S P L U K H
J D A P H F X A A J Q K G Q A Z Q F H O
```

LET'S DEFINE KEY TERMS! (page 33)

ANTIBLACKNESS—13 "The specific kinds of discrimination faced by Black individuals."

BIAS—8 "A disproportionate weight in favor of or against an idea or a thing."

DISCRIMINATION—11 "The unjust or prejudicial treatment of different categories of people or things, especially on the grounds of race, age, or sex. In other words: prejudice + action."

EQUALITY—12 "A state of fairness in which everyone has the same amount, despite their existing needs or assets."

EQUITY—4 "A state of fairness in which everyone has what they need in order to achieve that goal."

IMPACT—10 "The actual result of your words, actions, and efforts."

INTENT—7 "The desired result of your words, actions, and efforts."

INDIVIDUAL RACISM—2 "The beliefs, attitudes, and actions of individuals that support or perpetuate racism in conscious and unconscious ways."

INSTITUTIONAL RACISM—3 "Racist policies and practices that give unfair advantages to white people over people of color. These policies often never mention any racial group, but the intent is to create disparity."

INTERNALIZED RACISM—6 "The private racial beliefs held by and within individuals, usually absorbed via social, familial, political, and religious messages about race."

PREJUDICE—1 "A preconceived judgment about a person or group of people, usually indicating negative bias. (Also, really hard to spell.)"

PRIVILEGE—5 "The social advantages granted to and experienced by members of dominant groups at the expense of members of nondominant groups."

STRUCTURAL RACISM—9 "The overarching system of racial bias across institutions and society that systematically privilege white people and disadvantage people of color."

US CITIZENSHIP AND IMMIGRATION SERVICES TEST (page 63)

1. The Constitution

2. There are nearly 600 federally recognized tribes in the contiguous 48 states and Alaska. The official proctoring the test gets a partial list. Look up your answer!

3. Missouri, Mississippi

4. To print money; to declare war; to create an army; to make treaties

5. The one acceptable answer, per the US government, is "To stop the spread of Communism"

6. Virginia, Massachusetts, Rhode Island, Connecticut, New Hampshire, New York, New Jersey, Pennsylvania, Delaware, Maryland, North Carolina, South Carolina, and Georgia

7. The answers provided are "General during World War II; President at the end of (during) the Korean War; 34th president of the United States; Signed the Federal-Aid Highway Act of 1956 (Created the Interstate System)"

8. 27

9. 435

10. 6

11. James Madison; Alexander Hamilton; John Jay; Publius

12. Citizens eighteen (18) and older (can vote); You don't have to pay (a poll tax) to vote; Any citizen can vote. (Women and men can vote.); A male citizen of any race (can vote).

13. Franklin D. Roosevelt

14. "The Star-Spangled Banner"

15. Maine, New Hampshire, Vermont, New York, Pennsylvania, Ohio, Michigan, Minnesota, North Dakota, Montana, Idaho, Washington, or Alaska.

16. Vote in a federal election; run for federal office; serve on a jury

17. 1787

18. Depends on when you're taking the test! Look it up.

19. 9

20. Wow. So many to choose from, but acceptable answers include Light bulb; Automobile (cars, internal combustion engine); Skyscrapers; Airplane; Assembly line; Landing on the moon; Integrated circuit (IC)

GREAT* MOMENTS IN PRESIDENTIAL HISTORY (page 72-73)

A—1 Washington When this president ruined his teeth by cracking walnut shells, his dentures were made from the teeth of those he'd enslaved (along with cow and horse teeth).

B—16 Lincoln Known for being an antislavery hero and all, but in 1858 definitely said, "There must be the position of superior and inferior, and I as much as any other man am in favor of having the superior position assigned to the white race."

C—40 Reagan Ordered the US invasion of Grenada in 1983, authorized the CIA's trafficking of cocaine into the country, pretty much ignored AIDS, and relied heavily on race-baiting and dog-whistle racism, invoking "states' rights" and creating the "welfare queen" stereotype. Also a very mediocre actor.

D—30 Coolidge Was so opposed to the idea of government actually helping its citizens that he denied aid to the mostly Black riverside communities who'd been devastated in the Great Mississippi Flood of 1927 and refused to even visit the stricken areas.

E—7 Jackson Responsible for the deaths of at least 4,000 Cherokee people who were forced from their homes after he signed the Indian Removal Act of 1830.

F—13 Fillmore Signed the Fugitive Slave Act of 1850, making it legal to literally kidnap free Black people in the North and drag them back into slavery.

G—5 Monroe In 1823, he basically invented American imperialism with his own doctrine.

H—17 A. Johnson Considered by many to be the most-criticized president ever (well, until 2016). Drunk at his own inauguration after he accidentally became president, he wrote: "This is a country for white men, and by God, as long as I am President, it shall be a government for white men."

I—25 McKinley In 1898, after US forces overthrew the Kingdom of Hawai'i, he annexed it for the profit of white American farmers and businessmen. And tourists!

J—43 Bush "Brownie, you're doing a heck of a job." (History shows that Brownie indeed did not do a "heck of a job." Neither did this president.)

K—36 L. B. Johnson Passed critical Civil Rights legislation in the 1960s, but this good ol' boy from Texas was known for his frequent use of the N-word.

L—42 Clinton Signed the 1994 crime bill, accelerating mass incarceration by incentivizing states to build more prisons and hand out harsher sentences.

M—34 Eisenhower "At a White House dinner in 1954, this president shocked Supreme Court Justice Earl Warren when he said, "These [Southerners] are not bad people. All they are concerned about is to see that their sweet little girls are not required to sit in school alongside some big overgrown Negroes."

N—3 Jefferson Created an iterative algebraic equation to determine how long it would take to breed the Black out of someone, and said that "Blacks . . . are inferior to the whites in the endowments both of body and mind."

O—45 Trump Literally way too many shitty things to list about this one.

P—28 Wilson Took over Haiti! Resegregated the federal government! And the Navy! Publicly questioned the loyalty of "hyphenated Americans"! Stripped Black people from appointed positions of power and replaced them with white Southerners! Submitted a legislative agenda so racist his own Congress said "nope!" Held a screening for *Birth of a Nation* at the White House, which led to the resurgence of the KKK!

Q—11 Polk A lifelong supporter of slavery, he ruthlessly manifested America's racist destiny and in 1846 provoked war with Mexico.

R—44 Obama Labeled the "Deporter-in-Chief" for deporting nearly 3 million people during his eight years in office.

S—6 Adams Before he became president in 1825, he wrote in his diary, "Slavery in a moral sense is an evil; but as connected with commerce it has important uses."

T—32 Roosevelt Signed the 1942 executive order that forcibly imprisoned more than 120,000 innocent people of Japanese descent in internment camps.

MATH TIME! (pages 88–89)

WARM-UP: The solution is 1865, which represents the year the 13th Amendment was passed.

PROBLEM 1: The solution is 0.036, or around 4 percent (yes, this is a very small percentage). More than 42 million African Americans in the United States are descendants of this small percentage. Most enslaved Africans were shipped directly to the Caribbean and South America.

PROBLEM 2: 60 percent, or a total of 175,576 persons, were counted for representation.

PROBLEM 3: An estimate of 2,338,300 US prisoners.

PROBLEM 4: There were a total of 20 houses (or 1,000 residents) in the original neighborhood. 25 percent of original housing was demolished with the changes to the neighborhood.

PROBLEM 5: Answers will vary.

SKIN IN THE GAME (pages 120–121)

1. Larry Itliong—**E.** A Filipino American farmworker who led a 1965 strike of over 2,000 Filipino vineyard workers. He knew the real power lay in solidarity: Filipino and Mexican workers got pitted against each other by white growers, so he convinced Cesar Chavez and his union of Mexican farmworkers to join them. He did, and they became the powerful United Farm Workers.

2. Ralph Lazo—**D.** A Mexican American teenager who was outraged that his Japanese American friends were being forced from their homes and sent to prison camps in 1942—so he decided to go with them. He boarded a train to Manzanar, and spent two years as the only known non- Japanese person to be willingly incarcerated. He spent his life working for reparations for the Japanese American community.

3. Anne Braden—**F.** A white Southern woman who made headlines in 1954 when she purchased a home for a Black couple in a white suburb of Louisville, Kentucky. The house was bombed when neighbors realized the residents were Black. No one was charged for the attack, but Braden was charged with sedition and put on trial. She remained committed to racial and economic justice for life.

4. Viola Liuzzo—**B.** A white mother of five who heeded Dr. King's call for Northerners to join the fight for Civil Rights after Bloody Sunday. In 1965, she drove alone from Michigan to Alabama. She marched and organized for a month until she was murdered by a KKK member while driving with a Black man from Montgomery back to Selma. She was the only white woman killed during the civil rights movement.

5. Brad Lomax—**H.** A Black Panther organizer, and leader in the Disability Rights movement. In 1977, he helped lead over 100 disabled activists in the "504 Sit-In," America's longest peaceful occupation of a federal building. He rallied his Black Panther comrades to provide hot meals for the protesters every day. When he and 25 of the protesters flew to Washington, DC, to pressure Congress, the Panthers paid their way.

6. Barbara Henry—**A.** A white educator from Boston who was the only teacher willing to teach a Black child when her school in Louisiana was integrated in 1960. Her colleagues refused to teach, but she showed up every day to teach one student: six-year old Ruby Bridges. She was ostracized by the white folks in town, but she remained committed to teaching Ruby and keeping her safe.

7. Yuri Kochiyama—**G.** A Japanese American woman who began her antiracist work after being released from an internment camp and moving to Harlem with her family. A mother of six, she worked with diverse neighbors on social justice causes. She invited her friend Malcolm X to her home to speak to survivors of the Hiroshima atomic bomb. She was with him when he was murdered, and an iconic photo shows her cradling his head moments after he was shot. Their unlikely friendship transcended race and gender and shaped her radical activism for decades.

8. Grace Lee Boggs—**C.** A Chinese American activist who built multiracial working class coalitions and trained community organizers. She was so involved in Detroit's Black Power movement that her FBI file noted she was "probably Afro Chinese"—they couldn't understand why a Chinese woman be so committed to another community's struggle.

CROSSWORD ANSWERS

"FRUITS OF ONE'S LABOR"
(page 40)

SHUT UP AND DRIBBLE, MY ASS
(page 61)

SEPARATE AND NOT EQUAL
(page 77)

TELL IT LIKE IT IS
(page 97)

BLACK TO THE FUTURE
(page 147)

Acknowledgments

We did not create this book by ourselves—we created it with a community of artists, thought leaders, activists, scholars, editors, friends, and family. We'd like to thank and acknowledge:

Dian Holton is an art director and artist based in the Washington, DC, area. Her professional background includes editorial and publishing design, branding, retail installation, styling, and footwear design. Her passions include philanthropy, fashion, pop culture, travel, and amplifying underrepresented creatives!

Kelly Rafferty, PhD, is a writer, producer, and creative consultant whose work explores how political and aesthetic structures affect our everyday experiences of embodiment and connection.

Kenrya Rankin is an award-winning author, journalist, and editorial consultant who creates dynamic content that amplifies the lived experiences, advocacy, and work of people of color and shifts the narrative around who deserves liberation, justice, and dignity in America.

As well as:

Nathan Alexander, PhD, is an Atlanta-based teacher who explores the critical intersections between history and quantitative literacy.

Imani Love is an interdisciplinary writer and artist dedicated to Black storytelling and future imagining. You can find her by the water or yearning to be.

Alicia Garza is the author of *The Purpose of Power: How We Come Together When We Fall Apart*, a political strategist and principal at the Black Futures Lab and the Black to the Future Action Fund, host of *Lady Don't Take No* podcast, cofounder of the Black Lives Matter Global Network, and a cheeseburger enthusiast.

Juliana Tringali Golden is a crossword constructor and editor living in Oakland, CA.

Dr. Thanayi Jackson is a US historian whose research examines the politics of race and partisanship after the Civil War. She is currently assistant professor of history at California Polytechnic State University.

Dr. Nikki Jones is Professor and H. Michael and Jeannie Williams Department Chair of African American Studies at University of California, Berkeley.

Adesina O. Koiki is a veteran sports journalist—currently editor-in-chief of the sports website A Lot of Sports Talk—and crossword puzzle constructor for Vox.com.

Dr. Gabriel Mendes is the Director of Public Health Programs for the Bard Prison Initiative. Hailing from both LA and Brooklyn, he is the author of *Under the Strain of Color: Harlem's Lafargue Clinic and the Promise of an Antiracist Psychiatry.*

Sadie Red Wing is a Lakota/Dakota design educator and advocate for the Native American demographic in higher education.

Connie Wun, PhD, who has been practicing yoga for more than twenty years and is a student of Muay Thai, is also the cofounder of AAPI Women Lead and a national research consultant for projects related to race, gender, and state violence.

Special shout-outs to:

Itani Ramen, a ramen shop in Oakland, CA. Their food was essential to this book. We are actually waiting on an order as this is being typed.

Thundercat and **Hiatus Kaiyote**, whose music was pretty much the soundtrack to the writing of this book. It's playing right now, as we write this.

The visual artists:

Adriana Bellet (*pages 127, 128*, and *Centering Black Women's Voices*) is an illustrator who delights in painting spirited faces and colorful spaces. The iPad pro is her tool of choice, #fa2e04 is her current favorite color and lettering her newest fascination.

Chris O'Riley (*page 144*) uses CGI, photography, and digital retouching to provide visual content for advertising, editorial, and interactive media.

Favianna Rodriguez (*Envision the Future You Want, pages 150–151*) is an interdisciplinary artist, cultural strategist, and cofounder and president of The Center for Cultural Power, an organization that empowers artists to disrupt the status quo and ignite change.

Harkiran Kalsi (*pages 92, 93,* and *145*) is an energetic and exciting freelance graphic designer and illustrator who uses her art to bring positive vibes to and uplift people, and she uses her platform to shine a light on social injustices.

Hye Jin Chung (*pages 122 and 123*) is a New York–based artist whose cheerful, energetic temperament is expressed in the friendly and inclusive work she's become known for, with each playful illustration featuring bright, upbeat characters and well-dressed animals that march to their own tunes.

Hyesu Lee (*Big List of Actions You Can Take*) is a Brooklyn, NY, based illustrator, artist, muralist, and educator who is driven by a curiosity about how people connect. She was born and raised in Seoul, South Korea (and it's pronounced like "Heysu").

Jade Schulz (*pages 54, 55, and 120*) is an award-winning Korean American artist, illustrator, and designer mostly in Brooklyn, NY, and at other times in Ellicott City, MD.

Keisha Okafor (*pages 113 and Upstander*) is an illustrator who depicts joy and celebrates people in her work.

Kruttika Susarla (*pages 118, 119, and 125*) is an illustrator and graphic designer from Andhra Pradesh, India. She works on research-based fiction and nonfiction comics.

Marcus Kwame Anderson (*pages 7, 53, and all author caricatures*) is an illustrator, fine artist, and teacher who loves to tell visual stories.

Martin Gee (*pages 106 and 107*), #stopasianhate #blacklivesmatter + his work: ohmgee.com

Nicole Miles (*pages 5, 71, 94, 95, 116, and 117*) is an illustrator from the Bahamas, where it is warm and sunny, but she is now living in the United Kingdom where it is wet and windy with her pet snake and human boyfriend.

Paola Sorto (*page 53*) is a graphic designer born and raised in Maryland, with Hispanic roots thanks to her Salvadoran parents. She enjoys hand lettering, taking pictures of her dog Zoë, and finding new desserts to try.

Salini Perera (*pages 28, 51, and Talk To The Kids*) (she/her) was born in Sri Lanka, raised in Scarborough, and currently draws picture books for a living in Toronto, Canada.

Simone Martin-Newberry (*pages 29, 45, 49, 66, and 146*) is an illustrator and graphic designer who has created art for the *New York Times*, the *Guardian US*, Chronicle Books, Random House, and many others. Originally from Los Angeles, she currently lives, works, and gardens in Chicago.

Susana Sanchez-Young (*page 129*) is an art director for the *Los Angeles Times*. She has been operating her own consulting and design firm, the Designing Chica, from her home base in Walnut Creek in Northern California.

Therrious Davis (*pages 90 and 91*) is an illustrator based in Memphis, TN, who likes to tell stories and create work that ranges from themes of nostalgia and spirituality to pop culture and politics.

The folks who answered our community-sourcing calls for input, read the pages, and gave us invaluable feedback:

Jaha Alamgir

Judi Baker

Jenny Bergrenn

Jim Briggs

Sera Bonds

Tisa Bryant

Garrett Bucks

Soma Mei-Sheng Frazier

Melissa Garden

Liza Gesuden

Josh Healey

Tara Houska

Vanessa Hua

Adam Mansbach

Courtney M. Martin

Wendy McNaughton

Miranda Mellis

Sonya Mehta

Cava Menzies

Hindatu Mohammed

Renee Moreno

Sarah Jo Neubauer

Rachel Palacios

Jason Pontius

Joel Robinow

Virak Sarouen

Julie Scelfo

Lindsay Schlax

Kate Slater

Miriam Klein Stahl

Mira Stern

Leslie Dotson Van Every

Robbie Wilson

…and our social media friends, followers, and delightful trolls.

Above all, we thank:

Our committed and clear-eyed editors: Maisie Tivnan, Kenrya Rankin, Sun Robinson-Smith, and Analucia Zepeda.

And the design and production team at Workman Publishing: Janet Vicario, Orlando Adiao, Terri Ruffino, Kim Daly, Barbara Peragine, Annie O'Donnell, Elissa Santos, and Doug Wolff.

Our stellar team of agents and managers: Charlotte Sheedy, Sabrina Taitz, Sian-Ashleigh Edwards, Tim Sarkes, and Alex Murray.

Our beloveds:

Melissa Hudson Bell, PhD; Martha Rynberg; and Janet Cheatham Bell.

Lauren; the kiddos; Nancy Murray; and Barbara and Doug, aka Mom and Dad.

Our buddy Conan O'Brien, for using his platform for good and for doing his homework.

And all the writers, artists, scholars, and leaders who we cite and reference throughout the book: You've been doing the damn work forever and continue to teach and transform the world.

Privilege by the Numbers Sources (page 52)

White applicant callbacks: Quillian, Lincoln, et al. "Meta-Analysis of Field Experiments Shows No Change in Racial Discrimination in Hiring over Time." *Proceedings of the National Academy of Sciences*, 2017.

Weight-based discrimination: Puhl, R., Andreyeva, T. & Brownell, K. "Perceptions of weight discrimination: prevalence and comparison to race and gender discrimination in America." *International Journal of Obesity*, 2008.

Asian and Black job applicants: Kang, Sonia K., et al. "Whitened Résumés." *Administrative Science Quarterly*, 2016.

Black women with natural hair: Koval, Christy Zhou & Rosette, Ashleigh Shelby, "The Natural Hair Bias in Job Recruitment." *Social Psychological and Personality Science*, 2020.

Laws targeting unhoused people: Gus, Lindsay J. "The Forgotten Residents: Defining the Fourth Amendment House to the Detriment of the Homeless." *University of Chicago Legal Forum*, 2016.

Young adult homeowner: Choi, Jung, et al. "Millennial Homeownership: Why Is It So Low, and How Can We Increase It?" *Urban Institute*, 2018.

6% of homes physically accessible: Warnock, Rob, "How Accessible is the Housing Market?" *Apartment List*, 2020.

Elderly lesbian couples: Goldberg, N. G., "The Impact of Inequality for Same-Sex Partners in Employer-Sponsored Retirement Plans". UCLA: The Williams Institute, 2009.

AAPI and Latinx trans incomes: "Paying an Unfair Price: The Financial Penalty for Being Transgender in America." Movement Advancement Project and Center for American Progress, 2015.

Trans, genderqueer, and GNC students: Cantor, David, et al., "Report on the AAU Campus Climate Survey on Sexual Assault and Sexual Misconduct." Association of American Universities (AAU), 2015.

Indigenous women rape/sexual assault: Department of Justice, Office of Justice Programs, Bureau of Justice Statistics, American Indians and Crime, 1992–2002 (2004).

Black mental health diagnoses: Bell C, et al., "Misdiagnosis of African-Americans with Psychiatric Issues—Part II." *Journal of the National Medical Association*, 2015.

Indigenous adolescent depression: "Mental Health Disparities: Diverse Population." American Psychiatric Association, 2017.

Diversify Your Feed Sources (page 124)

14 out of 362 Black lead roles/8 out of 200 BIPOC actors: 2019 UCLA Hollywood Diversity Report, UCLA College of Social Sciences.

6% of writers/directors/producers are Black/Black talent funneled toward race-themed content: "Black representation in film and TV: The challenges and impact of increasing diversity." Report by McKinsey & Company, 2021.

Top-billed Latino/a characters/3% Latino-a directed: Smith, Staci L., USC Annenberg Inclusion Initiative, 2018.

Podcasts overwhelmingly white: Freiss, Steve, "Why Are Podcasts #SoWhite?" *Columbia Journalism Review*, 2017.

MENA characters: "Terrorists and Tyrants: Middle Eastern and North African (MENA) Actors in Prime Time and Streaming Television." MENA Arts Advocacy Coalition, 2018.

6 Black writers on 2019 NYT list: *New York Times*, 2020.

Children's books: Data on books by and about Black, Indigenous and people of color published for children and teens compiled by the Cooperative Children's Book Center, School of Education, University of Wisconsin-Madison.

"Big Four" publishing: So, Richard Jean and Wezerek, Gus, "Just How White is the Book Industry," *New York Times*, 2020.

Photo Credits

Permissions

STAY SAFE

- Go with a buddy and have a safety plan.
- Tell a friend where you'll be.
- Know who organized the protest.
- Check accommodations in advance: Safe for kids? ASL interpreter? ADA accessible? Restrooms?
- Be aware of your surroundings at all times.
- Have an exit strategy to get out of the crowd.
- Know where the cops are.
- Stay calm if things get heated.
- Leave if you feel unsafe.

- Bandanas soaked in milk/vinegar help you breathe through chemicals.

YOU HAVE THE RIGHT TO

- Peacefully assemble
- Photograph/film anything in plain view, including the police
- Protest in public spaces
- Distribute leaflets + literature
- Speak out on public property
- March in the streets/on sidewalks, as long as traffic isn't blocked
- Remember: Private property rules are different!

DON'T WEAR

- ✕ Valuable jewelry or watches
- ✕ Flip-flops, heels, or any shoes you can't run in
- ✕ Contact lenses—chemicals can get trapped behind them (if you have to wear contacts, bring protective goggles)

- Keep a "protest pack" stocked with sunscreen, snacks, water, tampons, First Aid kit, phone charger, etc.

- Comfortable, closed-toed shoes are best.

WHO Represents YOU

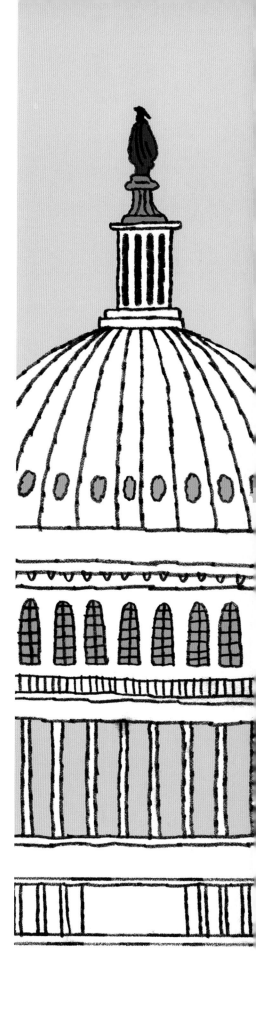

STATE

The Governor of my state is _____

Phone: _____

Email: _____

Next election: _____

The Attorney General is _____
and my Legislative Reps are _____
_____

Phone: _____

Email: _____

Next election: _____

FEDERAL

The two senators for my state are: _____
_____

Phone: _____

Email: _____

Next election: _____

Phone: _____

Email: _____

Next election: _____

I live in Congressional District _____,

and my elected Rep is _____

Phone: _____

Email: _____

Next election: _____

LOCAL

Since local government structures vary, fill in the ones you're most likely to want to contact!

_____

_____

_____

I WON'T STAND BY!

If I witness harassment, I can:

DISTRACT (De-escalate with an indirect approach)

DELEGATE (Get someone else involved)

DIRECT (Clearly state what's happening)

DELAY (Support the person who was harmed)

DOCUMENT (Take photos or video; share to social media)

If it's not safe for me to intervene, I can call:

_____

_____

_____

_____

More resources at: **ihollaback.org**

I WON'T STAND BY!

If I witness harassment, I can:

DISTRACT (De-escalate with an indirect approach)

DELEGATE (Get someone else involved)

DIRECT (Clearly state what's happening)

DELAY (Support the person who was harmed)

DOCUMENT (Take photos or video; share to social media)

If it's not safe for me to intervene, I can call:

_____

_____

_____

_____

More resources at: **ihollaback.org**

TO-DO LIST

I'M GOING TO

☐ **READ**

_____

☐ **WATCH**

_____

☐ **LISTEN TO**

_____

☐ **DONATE TO**

_____

☐ **LEARN ABOUT**

_____

☐ **GIVE A SHIT ABOUT**

REMINDERS

☞ **BRUSH + FLOSS MY TEETH**

☛ **WASH MY HANDS (WITH SOAP!)**

☞ **GET ENOUGH SLEEP**

☛ **STOP ACTING LIKE RACISM ISN'T MY PROBLEM, TOO**

☞ _____

☛ _____

☞ _____

☛ _____

☞ _____

TO-DO LIST

I'M GOING TO

READ

_____

WATCH

_____

LISTEN TO

_____

DONATE TO

_____

LEARN ABOUT

_____

GIVE A SHIT ABOUT

REMINDERS

BRUSH + FLOSS MY TEETH

WASH MY HANDS (WITH SOAP!)

GET ENOUGH SLEEP

STOP ACTING LIKE RACISM ISN'T MY PROBLEM, TOO

_____

_____

_____

_____

If it's not safe for me to intervene, I can call:

_____

_____

_____

_____

More resources at: **ihollaback.org**

I WON'T STAND BY!

If I witness harassment, I can:

DISTRACT (De-escalate with an indirect approach)

DELEGATE (Get someone else involved)

DIRECT (Clearly state what's happening)

DELAY (Support the person who was harmed)

DOCUMENT (Take photos or video; share to social media)

If it's not safe for me to intervene, I can call:

_____

_____

_____

_____

More resources at: **ihollaback.org**

I WON'T STAND BY!

If I witness harassment, I can:

DISTRACT (De-escalate with an indirect approach)

DELEGATE (Get someone else involved)

DIRECT (Clearly state what's happening)

DELAY (Support the person who was harmed)

DOCUMENT (Take photos or video; share to social media)

I DID THE WORK!

KIMBERLÉ CRENSHAW

DO THE WORK!

KEEP DOING THE WORK!

ANNA JULIA COOPER

END WHITE SUPREMACY

STAY HYDRATED & DON'T BE RACIST

DO THE READING

WHOSE LAND ARE YOU ON?

FUNNY BUT NOT F*CKING AROUND

REV PAULI MURRAY